THE EVOLUTION of the CUSTOM SCOOTER

By STUART OWEN

BANOVALLUM
BOOKS

Published in Great Britain in 2020
by Banovallum Books
an imprint of Mortons Books Ltd.
Media Centre
Morton Way
Horncastle LN9 6JR
www.mortonsbooks.co.uk

ISBN 978 1 911658 48 1

The right of Stuart Owen to be identified as the author of this work
has been asserted in accordance with the Copyright, Designs and
Patents Act 1988.

Typeset by BookEmpress Ltd., London
Printed and bound by Gutenberg Press, Malta

Dedicated to the memory of Paul Karslake

Acknowledgements

This book would not have been possible without all those people who have ever dared to alter the appearance of their Vespa or Lambretta at one time or another – thank you.

Thanks go to the following people who have contributed material and helped with this publication. Nicola Owen, Duncan Kilbride, Chas De Lacy, Andre Hill, Walter Nelson-Aylott, Kevin Corbett, Christian Schnieder, Colin Cheetham, Craig Derrigan, Damon Vaughn, Ian Wilkins, Dave Dickinson, Denbigh Mudge, Gary Wickham, Ian Bugby, Ian Johnson, Jason Taylor, Len Chandler, Mark Kendall, Dave Madison, Paul Dizzy, Rob Johnson, Paul Wood, Ralph Lowe, Nick Purser, Ray Stewart, Russell Watkin, Martin Murray, Pete Meads, Sean Wooden, Tony Miller, Michael Zinnen, Michael Zocker, Marc Leiskau, John Walklate, Frank Osgerby, Peter Ham, Jim Stretton, Dukesy Armillei and the Late Kevin Walsh.

Special thanks go to Jason Stephenson and Mark Brough for all their time and effort in making this happen.

Contents

Introduction

Custom scooters, now there's a big can of worms. When Stu asked me to do this introduction I jumped at the chance but then thought about it for a moment. Fair old task to be fair, a bit like painting the Forth Bridge; by the time it's finished someone will have raised the bar another inch or two! To do something covering custom scooters from as far back as the 50s sounded like sheer lunacy.

The scooter, simply by its original design, has always been a customiser's dream. A blank canvas, basic engineering, easy add-ons, easy take-offs and all that lovely panel work just begging to be painted or plated. I don't think for a minute that was intentional but once it left that factory it was certainly an open invitation to owners down the years. Who's to say whether it was the design or the fact that it predominantly became a vehicle for the young generation – a generation who not only wanted to belong but also wanted to stand out, turn a few heads and always cause a stir – that perpetuated the scooter custom phenomenon?

I've seen all manner of custom scooters over the years; being from sunny Scunthorpe has helped. I've even built a few but that was back in the day when it was easy, the days when the standard look was considered a bit 'last year'. One of the definitions of a 'custom' is that it's 'a personal styling statement' and there you basically have it in a nutshell! Scooters became style icons in what was essentially a style-driven youth movement. A pure expression of individuality within a scene that has encompassed all and where everyone is essentially riding the same vehicle is no mean feat!

It started back in the 50s/60s; the simple act of adding a rack, a mirror (or three), embellishers, mats, backrests, screens, mudflaps, non-standard seats, handgrips, bar-end tassels, whitewalls, crash bars, and Floridas, either because your mates had or because you fancied it yourself, was customising!

Since then each decade has seen something new. The 70s gave us electro-plating, home tuning, rattle can and then proper spray jobs, vreeble, crackle, metal flake paint, early airbrushed artwork/murals and signwriting. The 80s and 90s cut-downs, engine kits, engraving, endless custom themes, dedicated dealers and aftermarket specialists satisfying the need to do something just that bit different. The noughties galvanised the big name dealers and engineers, those with scooter scene backgrounds who took things to a new level. The painters and airbrushers strived to push new boundaries and the riders and owners scratched their heads to come up with something new, different and exciting.

I've often sat and thought about interesting and original custom themes, those that haven't been done yet, usually when a mate starts a new project or I see something new and exciting. Will we ever run out of ideas? I doubt it. You can almost guarantee that within a week someone somewhere will pluck something out of their 'twisted' minds and blow you away yet again. I can't think of any vehicle ever, considering its basic simplicity, that has been taken to such heights of customising than our old shopping trolleys. Long may that continue; I'm absolutely certain it will!

Best wishes to Stu with this book, he's a scooterist, he's been there and done it, so his angle comes from within; where better is there to seek inspiration? So anyway, enjoy the read and if you can't then just look at the pictures ha ha! Maybe, just for a laugh once you've done, rack your brains and name your top three all-time favourites. Now there's a task!

'Brad' (Mark Brough)
Author of Time Trouble & Money
Ex-Scunthorpe Roadrats SC – currently Scunthorpe Silhouettes SC

Chapter One

The Style Icons

No one can exactly say which was the first to make its debut in the UK, the Vespa or Lambretta. What is certain is that both brands would control and dominate the scooter market thereafter. To start off with they were seen as nothing more than a mode of transport, a cheaper alternative to what was on offer from competitors. Over time that sentiment changed somewhat and they became more than just that. Owners began to grow fond of the machines themselves rather than the purpose they were initially intended for. Before long local clubs and countrywide organisations began springing up everywhere to cater for their needs. It was starting to become a movement and almost a way of life to many. Attention was now focused purely on the scooter itself and this in turn meant owners were bound to begin making alterations.

There gradually came a noticeable change in how the scooter was perceived by the majority of owners. It seemed as though everyone was riding around on the same rather dull-looking machine. Not that anything was wrong with the Vespa or Lambretta; their exquisite Italian styling was way beyond anything else that was on offer. It could be argued that they were slightly different, depending on the colour choice from the factory. That was still very limited though and offered very little in the way of something that stood out.

As rallies and gatherings became more and more popular, it soon became apparent that owners were starting to put their own individual touches to their scooters. There was nothing too radical, mostly just the enhanced practicality of adding a carrier or fly screen. It was these small changes that began to make individual scooters look more unique. More than that, it was starting to create a bit of rivalry albeit a harmless one.

No longer did your scooter have to look exactly the same as the one you parked up next to and this made owners feel that their machine could be improved, certainly made different. This may have been light years away from the real era of customisation, but it was definitely the early beginnings of it. The word customisation is defined as the act of modifying something to suit a particular individual or task. Extensive customisation of an existing object could transform

A Vespa on display at the Earls Court exhibition in 1954. It is fitted with rather mundane accessories but interestingly the side panels are chrome

it into something totally new. It was that last statement which would have the greatest meaning and the most profound effect.

For now though, altering one's scooter would consist of nothing more than simple bolt-on extras. This trend did not go unnoticed by the manufacturers either, who were eager to sell owners as many aftermarket products as they possibly could. Both Vespa and Lambretta were already having accessories specifically made for their scooters, though the true potential of this initiative had not been fully exploited. Nevertheless, the manufacturers began to see it as a lucrative market that they had to cash in on. If they didn't, there were plenty of other outside companies waiting to do so.

It wasn't so easy to make accessories that would fit around the Vespa's wide bulbous body shape but the Lambretta, with its narrower and longer lines, was perfectly suited. It would lead to the latter being the one to benefit most from the surge in this new sector of the scooter market. Lambretta Concessionaires was by

A rally in London, again around 1954. All the scooters look exactly the same

now an established and successfully run company. Not only were they outselling virtually every other make of two-wheeled vehicle by the later 1950s, they were also selling aftermarket products in huge amounts to Lambretta owners. New accessories were coming out almost every week and a major part of the factory was now dedicated to the cause. This is where the individualism began to grow at a much faster pace. The more products that were made the more were sold and bolted onto owners' machines.

It was still possible for an owner to buy the same rack, for example, as the next person so they would still look identical when fitted. The difference was that now they would perhaps bolt a badge onto that rack to add their own touch. Soon this concept was transferred to the front of the scooter with the badge bar but was more prevalent with the fly screen. The Vespa was subject to this mode of modification just as much as the Lambretta. From the front, both makes could be transformed – which they were on an ever more frequent basis. Pendants were stuck on the fly screen from rallies attended or clubs joined and soon became emblazoned all over, to the point that the rider could only see directly in front of them. Badge bars were full of enamel plaques stating the county of origin or an association the owner was a member of. These were basic early forms of individualism that were the growing shoots of scooter customisation.

The Series II Lambretta would be the model that would break all records in terms of sales for Lambretta Concessionaires. It was at the peak of their market

A Lambretta scooter club in the mid-1950s on a local ride out. It is almost impossible to pick out one that is different from the others

As the decade moved on, changes to the scooter began to appear by way of accessories. Even so, they were still rather plain looking

domination – with tens of thousands now on UK roads. That is when the company came up with the idea of changing the colour of the scooters they had been sent by Innocenti back in Italy where they were built. Innocenti had offered the Series II with a very limited selection of colours to the horn casting and side panels and they were exported to the UK in those colours. The company had been doing this all the way back to the days of the LD so it was nothing new. Lambretta Concessionaires' idea was to offer a dealer an individual colour choice of their own choosing. It would still only apply to the same parts of the bodywork but at least it would be unique to that dealer and shop.

The thinking behind it was simple enough. From now on, any dealer would have the option to order a bright vivid colour as long as they had a certain number of machines painted the same. These would stand out when being driven around

The badge bar was an easy extra to fit on the front of any scooter. Owners began to fit plaques on them from their home county, which started to show they were different from anyone else

A fully accessorised Lambretta LD – which showed the scooter's true potential when it came to a change of appearance

locally and would be more noticeable to the public. It was thought that this high product visibility might entice new customers into purchasing one. With minimal outlay in labour and cost, the price of each individual machine would remain virtually the same. The initial plan was just raise awareness but it now had a knock-on effect that no one had even thought about. Owners were turning up at rallies with their Lambretta not only looking brighter but with different colours never seen before. More noticeably, this was factory paint – not some back of the garden or shed respray.

The idea of painting a Lambretta a different colour hadn't really been thought about much until now. Of course, it happened but definitely on older models with less value and not on a grand scale. Some machines had been on the roads for almost a decade and were probably beginning to look a little tatty by this time. It was usually a case of painting them over by hand. Now though, owners began to think that if the factory could change the whole look of a scooter then perhaps they could too – using more than just a tin of paint and a brush. This was an early catalyst of customisation and one that would move things forward very quickly. The Vespa with its monocoque frame was slightly different but also had removable side panels. So it too could also be subjected to the personal paint modification if so desired.

There were now other important changes happening as the 1960s dawned. Car ownership was slowly becoming a reality for many families. As it did so, the postwar two-wheeled transport boom slowly began coming to an end. The car would become the first choice of transport for many with the motorcycle or scooter a distant second. Though there were still good times ahead for the scooter, sales would, ultimately, shift to a younger generation of owners; those who would

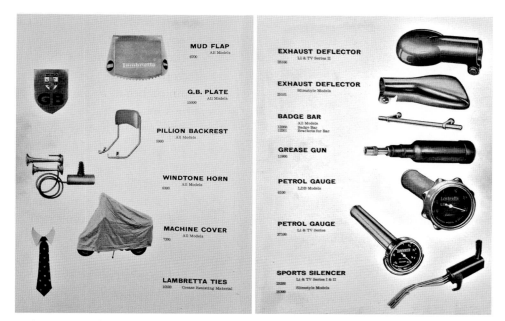

Just a small selection of the aftermarket accessories offered by Lambretta Concessionaires. This range would expand even further as the company began to see how lucrative it could be

see the scooter from more of a fashion perspective than anything else. These people would want to put their own unique mark on their machine. And doing so resulted in growing rivalry between owners, subjecting the scooter to change at a much faster pace than ever before.

What form this change would take was still the unknown quantity however. Owners were bolting bits on, adding pendants and perhaps spraying the side panels, but they were still a long way

Wind tone horns that were operated by foot soon became a popular addition to the scooter

from taking the whole machine to pieces and repainting everything. This is not surprising really as quite often Vespas and Lambrettas were sold through finance or HP as it was called back then. The idea of taking a new machine, that wasn't

Alpine horns were commonly used by mods years later

even going to be paid off for over a year at least, and radically altering it was not seen as the sensible thing to do. Perhaps that's why it was that older models began to have the real alterations made to them first. They were free from any finance and had less value – making them ideal for the purpose.

So it came as a bit of a shock when a new model was introduced called the Rallymaster. This was a purpose-built machine created by

By the turn of the decade, scooters were beginning to take on a more individual look as bars, racks, mirrors, lights and chrome began to take over

At the beginning of the 1960s customising began to move in new directions. Here not only repainting the bodywork but also removing parts of it

Lambretta Concessionaires and based on the Li 150 Series II. It was supposedly aimed at the sporting scooterist, which was a bit strange because at that time not much was happening in the form of racing or anything remotely like it. Featuring a two-tone black- and red-striped pattern on the side panels it certainly stood out. It also incorporated a turning style front mudguard like that of the Vespa. The engine was something of a first as the cylinder had been worked with what was claimed to be Stage 2 tuning. This was done in the engineering part of Trojan Works – a separate division to where Lambrettas were sold from. With a different set of gearbox ratios, it was the first purposely tuned Lambretta engine available on sale in the UK. Other extras offered included a dashboard which incorporated a Smiths rev counter among other things.

It was no racing machine and was a short-lived concept, probably due to its increased price. Lambretta Concessionaires never offered anything like it again. It was an important milestone though because it proved that modification could

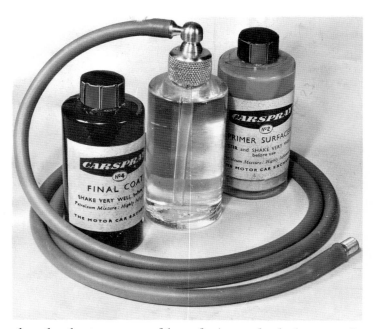

Though rather basic compared by today's standards, homemade paint spraying kits had entered the market – allowing anyone to have a go at painting their scooter

go way beyond what had previously been seen or even thought of. These were vital steps along the way to what would become real scooter customising, even if it was a manufacturer that had taken them before anyone else. All it needed now was for dealers who had the necessary skill and knowledge to take the idea on and do the same. One or two dealers were sufficiently entrepreneurial to realise what could be achieved. By offering something totally different they would have an advantage over their competitors. The market was still ultracompetitive and gaining an increased share of it was a difficult challenge. Offering something that rivals simply didn't have might be the answer. Some dealers were now thinking more than ever about going down this route.

By the beginning of the 1960s, the main Vespa was the GS and the main Lambretta the Series 2. Soon Innocenti would bring out a heavily updated model called the 'Slimstyle'. Though manufacturing commenced at the end of 1961 it wasn't really until 1962 that it became widely available, certainly in the UK. Its new streamlined design was a total transformation of its predecessor's wider bulkier look. It was obvious that those who already owned a Lambretta would want to update it for this new and far superior model. That would mean the Series II would lose its value pretty quickly. Soon those wanting a bargain Lambretta on the cheap would be able to get one, probably even with low mileage on the clock.

This also meant younger people on less income could now afford to buy one. And there was now another dimension added because they weren't new and were possibly a bit tatty here and there. Altering it in any way shape or form would be fine because there was no warranty to worry about breaking. Also, its value was only going to go down as new models were launched. It was almost as though owners had been granted a licence to alter their own machines and that's exactly what began to happen. Painting the bodywork was in vogue, as was removing it. Most commonly the front mudguard was removed, usually with the number plate reattached to the top of the fork loop. Sometimes the side panels were removed, which was a simple exercise. Exposing the engine and the front created a totally different look, but this was exactly what owners wanted. The cost was nothing – it was just a case of unbolting some of the bodywork. This wasn't going to be done

The dispatch bay of Lambretta Concessionaires at the height of Series II sales. At the front a group of Rallymasters, the first true custom Lambretta

to a virtually new 'Slimstyle' model, so owners of the Series II could make their machines look different knowing that those that had the new model probably wouldn't follow suit. It was a crude and cheap means of customisation but one that made their scooters stand out – which was exactly what customisation was about.

Painting your scooter was a more sedate affair and was still focused on the side panels and mudguards; basically, anything that was removable and easy to spray. Aerosol cans of paint now became more readily available and in more adventurous colours. Hanging a piece of bodywork up in the garage or shed and spraying it over was a pretty simple thing almost anyone could do. Soon older Lambrettas were appearing all over the place in a wide variety of colours. Some who were a bit more professional and had access to the right tools began to turn out some pretty impressive work. A change of panel colour with numbers painted on top also started to become a fashion. This was how the customisation revolution started to have a bigger impact. Owners were making mainstream changes which had a snowball-like effect. People were trying to make their scooters look different and changing them constantly, almost like fashion trendsetters.

The Vespa, unfortunately, seemed to get a little left behind for some reason. Probably because there wasn't such a change of models. The GS was still available until 1964 and had only been updated rather than superseded. The Lambretta had in the same time gone from the LD to the Series III so had seen far more rapid development, certainly in terms of styling. Because it was only the side panels that were removable on the monocoque frame, painting the bodywork was far more difficult to do. For now, customising the Vespa would still revolve around the bolting on of extras as that was still the easiest option. What was about to happen next would take the whole fashion and music scene by storm. At the centre of it all would be the Vespa and Lambretta and it would see them change like never before.

Chapter Two

Mirrors and Lights

The success of the Vespa and Lambretta could never have been predicted when they first landed in the UK but there was no doubt that together they had become a major institution by the early 1960s. Other manufacturers were practically forced to join the bandwagon for fear of losing out, but it was almost too late by the time they did. Many of them were motorcycle manufacturers and their idea was to simply encapsulate an existing model to make it look like a scooter. Many other brands borrowed an engine from somewhere else in an attempt to create something that resembled a scooter. Both Piaggio and Innocenti produced everything themselves including the engine. They were scooters designed and built as scooters and though different from one another couldn't really be bettered.

In the changing world of the early 60s, the scooter was going through a revolution just like everything else. As the age of universal ownership slowly evaporated, it became steadily more difficult for dealers to sell machines in the same large quantities that they had previously managed. The sales boom had peaked in 1959, when it was easy for a shop to shift in excess of 50 machines a week. Now it was far more difficult to achieve figures like that, so if they wanted to lure customers through the door they needed to come up with a new angle. Just offering accessories was not good enough any more; there needed to be something else. All shops had access to the same items and if anything the accessories market was almost at saturation point. To get one step ahead, unique ideas were needed.

Owners had started to make subtle changes to the paintwork of their scooters and it probably hadn't gone unnoticed by keen-eyed dealers. That seemed to be the best way to gauge the current trend – watching what the owners were doing then catering for their needs. The thinking by some was perhaps that it might be possible to create custom paint designs exclusive to their shop. That way customers would buy from them in the bid to have something different. This idea was still only a possibility though and it was almost as if no one dared to take the plunge for fear of getting it wrong. Besides that nothing else was really being offered, so it would only be a matter of time before at least one shop took up the idea.

An early scooter specifically made for scrambling. Based around a Lambretta LD it had many modifications that years later would appear on numerous custom scooters

An early version of the Mona dealer special based around the Vespa GS. This was one of the first scooters to have a custom paint job, which was offered by Glanfield Baldet

The thought of modifying anything else, such as the engine, was still a few years away. The Lambretta had the biggest engine with the TV 175 capable of 65mph – which was perfectly acceptable for traffic at that time. The potential to tune it was there but for the time being its performance seemed adequate enough.

The biggest worry many owners had was losing the warranty. Lambretta Concessionaires had a strict policy that if the engine was altered in any way then the warranty would be void. The Lambretta had a reliable engine but if someone took to their shed and tried to tune it then who knew what might happen? If anything did go wrong, then the customer would have to cover the cost. This thought was off-putting for most. Nevertheless, the Lambretta with its piston port induction and easy to work on engine was tempting to tune. Though it kicked out enough power there was far more just waiting to be extracted from it. The rewards were high but so too was the risk if it should fail.

Around the same time, the real teenage rebellion was beginning to build up a head of steam. The teddy boys of the 1950s were definitely the beginning, but by the early 1960s an exciting and vibrant new fashion was growing out of London.

It was based around a smart clean-cut look that centred around fashion and music. Known as modernism, it soon began to spread to other cities across the country. The mode of transport for the mod quickly became the scooter. The idea of the motorcycle with its oily chain and lack of weather protection did not have the same appeal. The scooter, however, was perfect; its clean lines and weather protection ideal when wearing expensive clothes and suits. Just driving around posing was what really mattered. There was no need to drive fast – so the scooter was the ideal choice.

Don Noys on one of his record-breaking speed attempts. His modified engine indicated that scooter tuning was beginning to happen

The mod ethic was not only to look smart but also to be individual and stand out from the crowd. That was done with clothes and hairstyles – which changed frequently. As soon as someone was seen wearing a certain type of clothing, others would follow suit and the instigator would move on to something different to stay one step ahead. With the Vespa and Lambretta being the preferred choice of scooter, they too began to get the same type of treatment. It's difficult to pinpoint exactly where it all started but it became noticeable that more and more extras were being bolted on. The easiest way to customise your machine was by fitting bars and racks and although there were plenty of different types it was still common for one scooter to look like the next.

Scooter customisation didn't seem to have any real direction at the time, even though a few were painting their scooters. To take it one step further certain mods began bolting extras on – but not off-the-shelf accessories. Now it was just about anything else they could find; lights, mirrors, car emblems, badges you name it. A lot of it centred around one thing and that was chrome, which looked bright and stood out. Scooters started to resemble peacocks that were proudly displaying their feathers. Before long chrome moved on to body panels, most notably the side panels and the front mudguard. Both the Vespa and Lambretta could benefit from this type of customisation as it was very easy to do. There were many spectacular creations and the latest craze in scooter fashion began to really blossom.

The Hurricane and Imperial offered by Grimsteads of London. Heavily modified Vespa and Lambretta custom scooters were now available

Something would start off in a small way – such as bolting a couple of lights or mirrors at the front of the scooter – and to better it, someone else would add a few more and then another even more. The excess became greater each time as owners tried to outdo one another. It didn't matter if the lights worked or not. The electrical power both the Vespa and Lambretta kicked out via their six-volt systems was nowhere near enough anyway. Fitting all that chrome had one objective – to stand out and look different from every other scooter owner. But all of a sudden, just like the flick of a switch, that idea became old hat and everything had to come off so that owners' scooters could be different once again.

It was this fierce competition that really began to take hold and change how each individual machine looked. For the first time, rather than bolt-on an accessory that was readily available, people were making changes according to their own ideas. This was the real beginning of scooter customising because it was the imagination of a person that was creating a style and nothing else.

Dealers it seemed were still slow on the uptake – they were just happy to sell new machines and trade second-hand ones. The first real and different offerings to come from any dealer began in late 1962. Francis and Woodhead were probably the first shop offering something for the Lambretta owner that no other dealer was. This by way of a tuning style more than anything else, with the emphasis on performance. For the Vespa, the introduction of the 'Mona' from Glanfield Baldet really stirred things up by offering a bespoke paint scheme. It could be argued that

**The Hurricane was heavily influenced by the mod look, which
by this time had peaked**

Grimstead's Hurricane

● Staggering acceleration, an increased top speed, and much greater top gear flexibility — these are the basic advantages of the Eddy Grimstead 200 Hurricane conversion kit when it is fitted to the standard 180 Vespa SS.

Grimstead's of Beehive Lane, Eastern Avenue, Ilford, London, specialise in marketing the Hurricane conversion as an extra on new 180 Vespas, although they do sell the component parts of the kit separately.

If you buy the new Hurricane, you get, in addition to the standard bike, the 200 cc conversion, a new recalibrated 100 mph speedometer, and a smart two-tone colour scheme. The extra cost over the standard mount is £7 0s. 0d. — but only on a brand new machine.

The bike we tested was second-hand, so we looked at the machine simply from the point of view of the conversion extras.

Undoubtedly, the biggest bonus lies in the increased acceleration. Blast away from a set of traffic lights and you could leave even the hottest of sports cars behind inside the first 100 yards.

The clutch had to be handled gingerly like a particularly hot potato if you didn't want to become airborne every time you started away from a halt, but once it was fully home the power surge was quite intoxicating and speed limits had to be watched very carefully.

Surprising flexibility

Perhaps the most surprising extra from this capacity bump-up was an altogether unexpected increase in all round flexibility. Torque was increased all through the range of engine speed, but nowhere was it more dramatic than right low down.

We test all bikes for their lowest non-snatch speed in top, which is the lowest speed from which they can be fully accelerated away without straining the engine. With the average bike, this speed lies between 20 and 30 mph. With the Grimstead Hurricane it was 12 mph. No-one was more amazed than our testers.

Top speed is only slightly increased however, with a little over 62 being the best we could obtain, although admittedly the engine was new and on the tight side.

The power fall-off once maximum revs had been obtained was not so sudden with the 200 as it is with the rest of the Vespa range. Economy, too was surprisingly good, with 80 mpg being easily obtainable with the minimum of careful driving.

The two-tone colour scheme add quite an eye-stopping patch of individuality to the machine, and also does a lot to cut out the bulbous appearance of the two rear blisters. The overall effect is to make the Hurricane look slimmer and sleeker than the standard model, but no-one complains about that.

The other unique extra is the 100 mph speedometer which is a Grimstead speciality. Only the most blissful optimist would ever expect the full range of this instrument to be ever needed, but the recalibration does give a much steadier reading in the middle section, and eliminates the vague wandering of the standard fitting.

External appearance of the enlarged barrel and head remains the same. Stroke is the same but bore up by 2mm.

The carburetter has a larger main jet but is otherwise standard. The size is upped from 117 to 120 on main jet.

Neat two-toning scheme is part of the Grimstead Hurricane deal. The colour panels on front give a slimmer look.

The Hurricane was one of the first dealer specials to be reviewed in the scootering press

this was the first true dealer special and was based on the GS model. A dealer offering something so unique was a big step forward. And it meant others would need to follow suit to keep up.

Whether or not this would be successful depended on how much more it would cost the owner. For most teenagers, purchasing by HP, any extra cost would put a scooter out of reach. Having said that, plenty were spending all their extra wages

Ian Johnson pictured with his Grimstead Hurricane on the way home from purchasing it and afterwards in Brighton

The Vespa GS as a mod scooter looked impressive and appealing to owners

on accessories so some possibly had the extra funds required. So why not channel those funds into a dealer special rather than loads of bars and chrome that would probably be discarded a few weeks after they were fitted? The problem for the dealers was how to get their products and ideas noticed. The only real outlets were *Scooter World* and *Scooter & Three Wheeler* magazines. Until the mid-1960s, both were just magazines reporting on general scootering topics and nothing much was covered when it came to customising and certainly not tuning. It was almost as if the magazines didn't condone this type of modification to scooters. At best, there would be a small picture with a two-line caption in the news section.

The Lambretta had a strong appeal even though many owners would go over the top with just how many extras they would bolt on to the bodywork

The Vespa 90SS introduced by Piaggio in 1966. With a tuned engine, dummy petrol tank and drop handlebars, it was the first true sports scooter offered by a manufacturer

There needed to be something more in the way of advertising and reporting these types of topics for any real notice to be taken.

Probably the first radical alteration of a scooter from an engineering point of view wasn't one based on customisation at all. Scootering scrambling was really beginning to take off and this required heavy modification to the frame. Most examples were based around the Lambretta LD and Series I models as there were plenty to go around and being outdated they were cheap as well. Most would have the bodywork unbolted but the biggest modification was the removal of the back of the frame. This was done just past the seat and rear frame grille and involved simply hacking it straight off. Although it would be another 20-odd years before doing this sort of surgery become fashionable – during the 1980s cut-down era – this was a major innovation in scooter customising.

For the first time bodywork wasn't simply unbolted, it was permanently removed and couldn't be put back. Owners had proven that they would go to whatever ends were necessary to make a modification. Scrambling became a popular sport for a while, with many Lambrettas been modified for the purpose. There wasn't much in the way of tuning the engines as top speed wasn't essential. What was altered was the exhaust as it was too low to the ground in standard form. Most would simply cut the downpipe in half then reweld it upright, so the box section would go over the engine. Again, this style wouldn't reappear until a few years later when scooter racing took off.

Even as scooter scrambling became popular the modernist movement began to slow down, certainly in the mainstream, once it was made commercial in 1964. The riots at seaside resorts didn't help much either and the two combined to begin killing the fashion off. There were still many young scooters owners out there but without all the competition of one-upmanship, the changes wouldn't come so fast. Soon all the mirrors and lights were being removed rather than added as the scooter went back its familiar look. The bolt-on extra idea had gone way

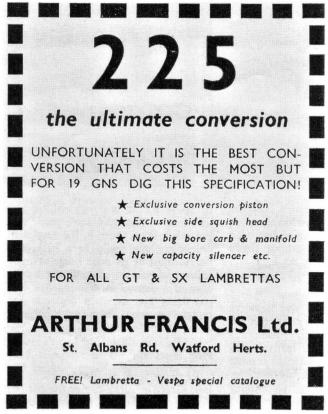

An advert by Arthur Francis Ltd for a 225cc conversion for the Lambretta. At the time this was the biggest being offered

Comedian Frankie Howerd sitting on an SX 200 dealer special. This is where the classic mudguard stripes on the paintwork first appeared

over the top – with some scooters almost buried underneath a sea of chrome extras. The moment it was out of vogue it was all gone, left to rot in the back of garages. There were still mods around, and the fashion would have its place within the scene throughout the 1960s, but the quick impact it made had now faded.

As the decade moved on it was the dealers themselves who would start to dictate and control how the scooter would look and what form future customisation would take. By now Francis and Woodhead had become Arthur Francis Limited and it was Arthur himself who would begin to change things for the Lambretta. In 1963, the TV 200 had been introduced into Britain by Innocenti – the first 200cc Lambretta in the world. Arthur was keen

A later incarnation of the Mona dealer special once the SS180 Vespa had been introduced

to cash in on its popularity and therefore launched his own custom variation of it with the 'S Type'. It came with all sorts of optional extras including 12-volt lighting, Smiths chronometric speedometer and spotlights on the front. More importantly, it came with a two-tone paint job and a tuned engine. These were dramatic developments which thrust Lambretta customisation into the spotlight.

By 1966 the 'S Type' had become even better with the launch of the SX 200 and soon after a 250cc conversion was being offered. This was created by grafting a Bultaco motocross cylinder to the casing. It was a complicated procedure that was impractical and certainly uncommercial but a great marketing exercise. It also showed just how extreme modification to the Lambretta could be if you put your mind to it. By 1967 scooter owners had started to move away from the bolt-on modification ethic, with engine tuning and performance starting to gain precedence. Hot on the heels of Arthur Francis was a new shop which had

A sports screen and fairing offered by Don Noys through Nannucci Accessories. It didn't do much for the looks and was a short-lived idea

WILL YOU SETTLE FOR LESS THAN BEST?

PERFORMANCE PLUS PROVEN RELIABILITY

1. Snetterton 12 hour speed trial. Overall winners Norman and John Ronald (Nottingham)

Riding Arthur Francis SX200 'S' type.

PERFORMANCE PLUS PROVEN RELIABILITY

2. Avon Valley champion, second overall Western 250. Mike Kemp (Hitchin)

Riding Arthur Francis Vespa 110 ('90') sprint

PERFORMANCE PLUS PROVEN RELIABILITY

3. From Lambretta Concessionaires to Milan (home of Lambretta) 700 miles in 16 hrs. 50 mins! Ken Peters (Cambridge)

Riding Arthur Francis SX200 'S' type.

exclusive Vespa & Lambretta agent — for discriminating riders only!

Arthur Francis Ltd., St. Albans Road, Watford, Herts.

● SEND FOR FREE CATALOGUE ●

Attention to advertising switched to what riders were doing in competition, with Arthur Francis being very successful

The Arthur Francis S Type was becoming a successful brand and could be based on any model of Lambretta, in this case, the SX 150

Practical Scooter **magazine was ground-breaking in showing just what could be done when it came to customising the scooter**

opened in 1966. It was called Supertune and as the name suggests it was all about engine performance. The owner, Malcolm Clarkson, believed this was the way forward for the Lambretta and soon began to create some exciting new styles and developments.

One of these was called the 'low line' which for the first time offered a major frame modification to a road-going machine. The front forks and leg shields were shortened by just over 3in to give a much sportier look. Finished in black with Y-shape motif on the side panel and white stripes on the front mudguard as well as the V line of the horn casting, it gave a totally new and fresh look to the Lambretta. The engine was tuned and though still using the traditional cast iron cylinder it boasted 235cc. It was seemed like bigger was better when it came to the Lambretta engine, but owners liked it. Intake was either via the Wal Phillips fuel injector or the newly launched Amal MK 1 concentric carburettor. The fuel injector was a crude device and without a float chamber almost impossible to set up without flooding the engine. But when it did work, even without any additional tuning, acceleration was improved though probably not as much as the bold claims that were advertised. The Amal was far better suited as it was a conventional

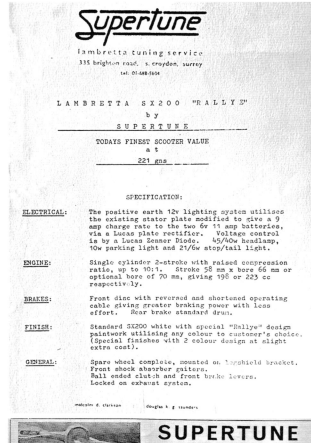

Supertune of Croydon offered a heavily modified Lambretta both in terms of performance and finish. It was adverts like this that made owners think about just what could be possible when it came to customising their scooter

carburettor. It wasn't directly aimed at the Lambretta and was intended to supply the UK motorcycle manufacturers. However, it would fit on a Lambretta quite easily with the correct manifold which was now being cast. Its simple set up complemented a tuned cylinder very well and showed the true potential of the 200cc Lambretta engine.

Another addition to this style of early tuning was the big bore exhaust. This had first been championed by Arthur Francis himself. The standard downpipe on the Lambretta engine was 38mm and the big-bore variation increased this to 42mm. The inlet into the box section of the exhaust was far bigger by way of a tapered cone. Though no huge gains were made it was an improvement and was necessary if cylinder tuning and a larger carburettor were to be added. It was mounted in exactly the same place on the engine so it was very easy to fit – a real advantage. Before long, Supertune had its own version and bigger too with a 48mm downpipe. The result was the beginning of very welcome competition between companies.

Personalising a scooter could be as simple as adding vinyl stickers, but it worked

Though the mod fashion had died out towards the end of the 1960s some scooters would still be decked out with bars and racks by their owners

Don Noys, who had been a Lambretta dealer, was attempting various speed records and this finally began to wake up the scooter press. At the same time he had been put in charge of a company called Nannucci Accessories, which made aftermarket products for both the Vespa and Lambretta. Having heard of the Ancillotti brothers breaking various speed records in Italy on a Lambretta, he invited them to England in late 1966 to do the same. This was reported in the scooter press – most notably because they broke a speed record at Elvington airfield in North Yorkshire. This gave Nannucci some free publicity along the way and Noys was keen to capitalise on the tuning skills of the brothers, so he set up a deal to sell their products. This included their version of the big bore exhaust and a production cylinder kit based on the original Innocenti Lambretta barrel. Now there were several companies selling tuning accessories for the Lambretta, which would only encourage more to join in over time.

On the Vespa side, things weren't heating up quite as much but London-based scooter dealer Eddy Grimstead played his part in trying. He offered a similar style of customising for the Vespa with a tuned engine and different paintwork styles. The idea with the paint was that the owner could choose the colour and according to certain adverts there were more than 1000 different colour options. Perhaps that was a bit of an exaggeration but it proved a good way to lure customers into the shop.

The offer was for the Lambretta too, which was unusual because normally you either stocked the Vespa or the Lambretta, not both. The range had been available for a while and was named the 'Imperial'. When it first appeared, it was made up of bolt-on accessories such as bars and seat covers etc. As time went on so too

The side panel removed from a Vespa revealing the spare wheel. It showed it would look odd if they were left off, unlike the Lambretta

did the look – changing more towards a sport orientated style. Piaggio itself also shook the market with the introduction of the 90SS: a 90cc small frame Vespa with a tuned engine and performance to match. With a dummy petrol tank in the same position as you would find one on a motorcycle, it certainly looked different. Completed with a drop handlebar headset, it proved the manufacturers weren't scared of making radical changes. The tank and headset idea would become fashionable in scooter customising decades later but the influence must have come from this Vespa.

Something else important for the world of customising scooters happened in 1967 and this could have been the catalyst that accelerated it more than anything had before. Until then, the only way of knowing about what these new style scooter shops were doing was either by living locally or hearsay. *Scooter World* magazine was only the only mainstream publication by this time but it still seemed trapped in its mundaneness and was failing to report on this part of the scooter scene. A new magazine made its debut in 1967 called *Practical Scooter and Moped*. It had a completely different approach and seemed to only want to feature articles on

The Series II Lambretta by this time was well outdated and cheap to purchase. Customising it by repainting wasn't going to alter its value much. The SX 150 might have the odd part painted and a big bore exhaust added but nothing else

scooters that were different. It wasn't interested in the traditional road test reports or the latest places to go touring. Totally the opposite: it went all-out on engine tuning, customising paintwork and reports on the latest radical dealer specials. It was a breath of fresh air and opened up a new world to many scooterists.

The likes of Arthur Francis and Supertune for the Lambretta and Moto Baldet and Eddy Grimstead for the Vespa had all their latest creations featured. More than that, the front cover was colour and apart from titles on the side the whole of the page would exhibit one of the said scooters. It was a revelation and showed the owner just how much you could alter your scooter if you so desired. It was basic by today's standards but these were the pioneering days of customisation and *Practical Scooter and Moped* was no doubt a big influence and broke new ground when first published. There was only one problem with the magazine – it didn't sell very well. Perhaps it was too radical, and owners didn't know what to make of it. After just 12 editions, at the end of 1967 it disappeared. Luckily it had left a footprint for others to follow and it did seem to have shaken up *Scooter World* magazine which started to get more adventurous with its reporting on such subjects.

The late 1960s was a strange time for the world of scooters. Innocenti launched its new model at the beginning of 1969. By the time it did so the company was beginning to struggle and its future was in doubt. Piaggio had relied on the SS 180 for a while but this was replaced in 1968 by the Rally which was the company's first 200cc scooter. The new Lambretta, like its predecessors, was still a 200cc variant and similar technically. What it did have was much sleeker and sportier styling thanks to the endeavours of Bertone. It was only a revamp of the SX 200 bodywork but it gave the Lambretta a much more modern feel and look.

By the time both had been launched the idea of multiple mirrors and lights was becoming a real thing of the past. There would be times in the future when the idea would be resurrected but for the time being, it was definitely out of fashion among the mainstream of owners. Attention now began to switch more and more to engine tuning. This was fuelled by the interest in scooter racing which was really starting to pick up as the decade came to a close. Tuning was an important part of scooter customising because when owners modified their engines it seemed natural that the rest of the machine would need upgrading to match. And when racing teams were formed they wanted to look different from one another so spraying scooters in a different colour became a priority. These were the two main ingredients that went into making a custom scooter. Surely this would equate to exciting times ahead in the 1970s.

Chapter Three

A Faster Approach

With the beginning of a new year there is always optimism about better things to come. The effect is greater still when welcoming in a new decade. The 1960s would be a hard act to follow and for scooter owners things were going to drastically change.

By now all two-wheeled sales had dropped significantly as the car took centre stage when it came to travel. For Lambretta owners, the GP had been an instant hit and sales were strong despite the general downturn. It was no surprise as the updated design of the bodywork made it so appealing. With the power increased slightly over the SX 200 it performed better too. Even though the official top speed claim by Innocenti was 69mph, in reality 70mph was possible with the right conditions. With a little bit of tuning – perhaps even just adding a big bore – that figure could be pushed even higher. Owners realised that if Innocenti had produced what was labelled a sports scooter then surely it could be made even faster. With tuning now very much in vogue, shops that catered for this needed to take advantage.

The advent of 1970 was not only the beginning of a new decade, it was also the beginning of a new era in scooter racing. It would see the first season of a full national championship, and this was gaining many entrants. Though Vespas would be raced, the sport was dominated by the Lambretta. Even brand-new GP models would be used by some once they were run in. This proved even more that scooter ownership was in the hands of the teenage generation – those prepared to take the risk of damaging their scooter if it crashed during a race, regardless of the consequences.

As the sport rapidly grew many teams began to form from all parts of the country and each wanted to stand out from the competition. This meant painting the scooters in different colours and adding a race number on the side – possibly along with the team logo or the rider's name. Soon all sorts of different shades of paint began to adorn Lambretta bodywork. Even brand-new GP models in some cases would go through the same treatment. Many owners who went to watch the racing would be influenced by what they saw. Race scooters looked smart and

Many owners were now doing the tuning work themselves despite their machines looking fairly standard. The Amal MK I carburettor was a popular choice with a 225cc conversion

sporty and combined with their tuned engines they not only looked fast; they actually were.

Many shops realised that now was the time to cash in on what was happening – and more importantly so did Lambretta Concessionaires. During the 20 years since the company had been established it had always taken a harsh line on any type of modification to the engine. Warranties would be voided with immediate effect if it was altered in any way, shape or form. Yet not only was Lambretta Concessionaires now offering performance upgrades to older models by the way of the cylinder and carburettor improvements, it was even producing its own tuning handbook. No publication like it had ever been seen before and it opened up the door for those with older Lambrettas to go faster.

It was no longer exclusive just to the GP and because the engine layout had remained the same for such a long period it was easy to achieve. And it went further than just tuning products as sports seats and racks also became popular. Some shops even started to offer spray paint in aerosols in a wide range of colours. There

A typical clubman style Lambretta, which was becoming more popular. Humpback style seat, reverse pull front brake and ball end levers were subtle but important changes

The GP was a clever revamp by Bertone of the SX series Lambretta. No one could have imagined even 50 years on how much it would influence the custom scooter scene

was finally a realisation that owners were prepared to paint their own scooters – however amateurish such a paint job might prove to be. Even the SX 200 was considered an old outdated model by this time so if you had one, why not change its appearance? With its second-hand value at rock bottom it didn't matter if its appearance was altered.

All of what was going on paled into insignificance in the spring of 1971 as Innocenti shocked the world. It was taken over by the then ever-expanding British Leyland – the company that had evolved out of BMC. The move had been on the cards for while due to Innocenti losing its direction plus the crippling union strikes of 1969 known as the 'hot autumn'.

Once British Leyland had taken over, it was quick to change things around at its new acquisition. The real reason it had wanted Innocenti was to have a factory in the middle of Europe from which it could build its cars. This was seen as a better way to access the European market than by exporting cars made in Britain. Innocenti had been producing cars under licence for BMC for over a decade, so it was seen as an easy switch. With this in mind, the sole focus was purely on cars and the first decision of the new owners was to halt production of the Lambretta.

The remaining assets and rights relating to the GP were sold off to India. The management had decided that anything two-wheeled was part of a dying industry.

There was no time for affected parties such as Lambretta Concessionaires to try and persuade them to think otherwise. In effect, the Lambretta scooter was finished and consigned to history. Perhaps the decision was a bit hasty but there were other factors that had had a bearing on this fateful decision.

The style and look of the GP couldn't be argued against but its technology was well outdated by this time. The Series I Lambretta had been introduced in the 1950s and the same engine layout, along with the same brakes and suspension, were still being used. It had been updated here and there but nothing had significantly advanced. British Leyland probably realised that if it wanted to keep up

Jim Muir with his brand-new GP in 1971. Even though it is only a few weeks old it already has a tuned engine, a number on the side panels and was being raced at tracks around the country

Racing scooters were subject to rather extreme modification. Cutting down the frame and bodywork may have been for practical purposes, but these changes soon became a style influence

Only a few years old, this TV 200 was subject to extreme use – showing how the value of the Lambretta had dropped by the early 1970s

with the Japanese motorcycle manufacturers it would need to heavily invest in revamping and overhauling the Lambretta. To Innocenti's new owners, it was a huge financial risk not worth taking and although a great brand was being brought to an end the company was in fact making the right decision.

Like any vehicle when production stops, the value of every Lambretta scooter crashed at the moment of the announcement. Even fairly new GP models rapidly lost value and dealers tried their best to offload stock new or second-hand as quickly as possible. This meant there were some real bargains to be had, making top of the line Lambrettas affordable to teenagers. Just like the LD and the Series I before it, even the GP could be had for a song. This also meant that if you wanted to alter your scooter's appearance the value wasn't going to drop as the second-hand market quickly became saturated. The Lambretta had fallen from grace as a mode of transport for the masses. Now though it was about to enter a new world – taking it to levels and extremes never seen before.

The Vespa hadn't suffered the same fate – probably due to the management at Piaggio being better at controlling its finances than Innocenti. With production still ongoing and stabilising, if anything, despite the general industry decline, the Vespa was here to stay. One thing Piaggio didn't do was invest heavily in development. The Vespa was a reliable and stylish looking scooter and in Rally 200 form it was a powerful machine. As long as sales continued to be strong enough there was little point in spending huge sums on a new model and production line.

Consequently, the price of a Vespa would remain much higher than that of the Lambretta. Also, if you still wanted to buy a new scooter then this would be the only choice from now on. For years owners had always seemed to have an allegiance to either the Vespa or Lambretta, so if you were in the latter camp you would have no choice but to switch if you wanted a new machine. While people

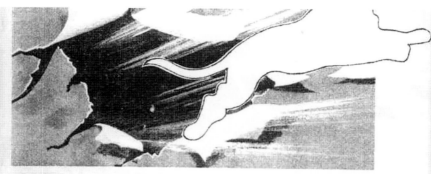

THE GREAT LEAP FORWARD!
OUR "WILDCAT" ENGINEERS
HAVE NOW PERFECTED ONE OF
THE MOST "ADVANCED
MODIFICATIONS" AVAILABLE
AS AN EXTRA.

"5 PORT INDUCTION."

What is 5-Port induction?

Normal 2-Stroke engines have one inlet port, and two transfer ports
for induction. Our new 5-Port barrel has these PLUS two extra booster
ports, designed to increase flexibility and performance by up to 30%.

The efficiency of a standard two-stroke engine is impaired by lingering
exhaust gases at the piston crown, the two extra booster ports clear
these gases with a further charge of fresh fuel, thereby not only
thrusting the burnt gases out but increases the thermal efficiency,
with a cooler running piston and an improved combustible mixture.

WILDCAT 5-Port Scooters (model X5) are available for as little as £20
over current list prices. Outwardly these Scooters will resemble
standard models, which will obviously add to the excitement of owning
and riding a machine unbeatable in its class!

Many other features can be added, if required, such as Ancilotti racing
seat and any other accessory listed, which will, of course, alter the
prices accordingly. Two tone finish is also available to any colour
required, in fact we can build a machine to YOUR Specification, the
price of which is determined by your requirements.

Also available is a Works WILDCAT Scooter fully equipped with 5-Port,
special works racing piston, Ancilotti seat, and modified lighting
all for £45 over current list price.

260-262 WEST STREET, FAREHAM, HAMPSHIRE, ENGLAND

Telephone: Fareham 1649

**A breakthrough in Lambretta tuning according to Rafferty Newman with
the five port Lambretta cylinder. Tuning was the only real way forward for a
scooter business eager to drum up trade**

12 / AF / 71
superseding
all previous
leaflets.

tune it!

for Lambretta Series 2, slimstyle and Grand Prix models.

Our stage 4 tuning is the ideal. On a mechanically sound engine the admitted extra stress if using the performance consistantly will have negligable reduction in the life of the unit. Tuning should not be entertained to obtain performance lost to below standard output, through incorrect, or insufficient maintenance, the worst offender points - timing. If your Lambretta is rough, spend the money getting it right, then have the tuning to get above standard acceleration and speed.

The ultimate is with a Large Bore Clubman exhaust, and a larger carburettor, but electronic tests with a stage 4 tune on a standard carburettor and exhaust gave a genuine 6 miles an hour on top speed, and greatly improved acceleration. With a Racing Large Bore Clubman exhaust and 30mm carburettor, a Grand Prix 200 with full panelwork has exceeded a genuine - not tuned speedometer - 86 miles an hour.

STAGE 4 TUNE We require barrel, piston, head, induction manifold.

The components are immersed in a non corrosive cleaning agent, checked for wear and if within tolerances the following effected. Exhaust port raised, profiled and polished. Transfer ports modified, and blended. Induction port and manifold matched and polished. Cylinder head skimmed, shaped and polished. (200cc models pre number 854000 with central squish head are advised to replace it with side squish type, additional £2.50).

125cc ..... £9.00   150cc ..... £8.50   175cc £7.50

200cc ..... £7.00   225cc £6.50

If sending by post, pack carefully. For return registered post, send further 85p.

ADVICE COSTS MORE THAN YOU THINK!

We have opened an ADVICE BUREAU FOR LAMBRETTA OWNERS. There are not many queries from maintenance, to advanced tuning that we cannot answer, we have the services of outside consultants should there be something on which we get into difficulties. We require as much information as possible about your machine, symptoms of troubles, model and year, of course, mileage, any non standard work effected or parts fitted, and a postal order, or cheque for 25p. Sorry, but wages, light, heat, paper and postage has been assessed by an expert to a city firm as an invoice sent out costing almost 50p - and we are offering a comprehensive technical service.

Arthur Francis Ltd offered a different angle with stages of tuning. This would become a major part of the custom scooter scene in the 1980s, with Stage 6 as the must-have requirement for most

Fred Willingham, the legendary tuner and sprinter, pictured with his record-breaking Lambretta. He would write a series of articles on how to tune a Lambretta that many owners would use as a guide

SCOOTER WORLD
AND LIGHTWEIGHT MOTORCYCLE

SEPTEMBER 1971

In this issue

Full
Photographic
Coverage of
Mallory

Road
Test of
Suzuki
Cat

Readers
Pics.
DKR Defiant
Sun Wasp
Lambretta D

15p

Scooter World **magazine had been around since the 1950s but by now it concentrated on scooter performance modifications**

would bolt on extras to the Vespa as they had done in the past, radical changes were still a while away. It was important to still have the availability of a new scooter; if the Vespa had suffered the same fate there would only ever have been a declining market. Though this was perhaps not so important at the time, in future years it would have a significant impact on scooter ownership numbers.

For now, the Lambretta was your first choice if you wanted a scooter that could be altered for the road or the race track. With the Lambretta finishing production, some doubted that the race scene would survive. In fact, the complete opposite happened. Not only did there seem to be a never-ending supply of machines but spares as well. It must be remembered that tyre technology was nowhere near what it is today and falling off going around a race track was an accepted part of the sport. With replacement machines and spares now considerably cheaper, scooter racing all of a sudden was a much cheaper sport overall. There seemed to be two main aspects to altering the Lambretta for race use and these were undoubtedly a huge influence on customising the scooter in later years. The main area was the engine itself, which would need tuning for more speed and performance. There

Race scooters were now showing different aspects when it came to the paint and when done right they looked impressive – a definite forerunner to the street racer concept

were plenty of shops now offering conversions and developed parts along with individual owners who had tuning knowledge.

These people would do the work in their own garden sheds or garages. As general dealers around the country dumped the Lambretta brand, the shops that now catered for them were more specialised and tuning products became the staple part of their business. They were very localised when it came to a customer base and those that purely supported the Lambretta were the ones that would struggle. By the early 1970s, the likes of Supertune were already gone and even Arthur Francis Ltd was finding it hard going. Others such as Rafferty Newman with its Wildcat tuning range would diversify into the motorcycle market and even thrive as the Japanese invasion began to take hold. This meant that they could continue to develop the Lambretta engine and sell related products – but the firm wasn't dependant on scooters to remain afloat. It was hard work and one of the biggest shops to cater for Lambretta tuning, Roy's of Hornchurch, knew this all too well. Owner Roy Cary always maintained that it was almost impossible to make a profit solely out of the Lambretta by the 1970s.

The Concessionaires in this country ensured continuity by importing new machines from Spain months before the Italian supplies were exhausted, but the only models from there are versions of the SX150 and SX200. This is a disappointment to us, as we consider that the discriminating 'S' type customers will be reluctant to have this work effected on the earlier styling than we have known with the Italian Grand Prix, and we have reluctantly decided not to proceed with the Arthur Francis 'S' type models at least until there has been a year to better assess the situation - or earlier if the Spanish give a Grand Prix face lift to their products, which is wishful thinking, but the much increased sales to this country must at least bring forward their next re-tooling date.

A statement from Arthur Francis Ltd about suspending production of the S Type due to the GP not being available any more. These were worrying times for the scooter scene during this period

SPECIAL NOTE.... ALL ITEMS ARE SENT "POST FREE (WITH THE EXCEPTION OF CONVERSIONS) — TO ANY PART OF THE U.K. — WE REGRET WE ARE UNABLE TO ACCEPT C.O.D ORDERS.

Rafferty Newman would champion the postal system to get its products to Lambretta owners around the country. A vital link for keeping the tuning market going

By the mid-1970s, even a GP that was only a few years old would be totally resprayed as owners really began to put an individual mark on their scooters

Aftermarket products for the engine centred around the carburettor and the exhaust. These could be bought directly by the customer and could be instantly bolted on to the engine. They offered by far the biggest and easiest gain to be made in performance. Internally, things such as barrel tuning and cylinder head and crank modifications came specifically down to what each individual shop was prepared to offer. There were no manufactured cylinder kits as such because the market at this point simply wasn't big enough to warrant the manufacturing costs. Nannucci had tried it for a while but even they were now out of the market. Someone with good two-stroke tuning knowledge and engineering skills could create quite a powerful engine at home. Whenever this happened, and the local Lambretta fraternity came to hear about it, the home tuner's house would be besieged by those who also wanted to go faster.

All of this was still being fuelled by *Scooter World* magazine, which by now was the only publication left specifically for the scooter owner. There were homegrown offerings such as *Club and Circuit* magazine but these were only sold at race meetings so they didn't make much impact due to limited availability. With the Lambretta gone and the Vespa line devoid of new models, the racing scene was all that remained to report on. Every meeting, whether it was circuit racing, sprinting or off-road trials seemed to be covered in *Scooter World*. Now too the editorial staff included legendary Lambretta tuner Fred Willingham. His exploits in getting a Lambretta to go over 100mph had not gone unnoticed and he was quickly hired. In a series of articles, he gave away the secrets of his success with the Lambretta engine. This was combined with general tips on improving performance and as the main adverts within its pages came to be mostly for tuning products, the magazine almost became a tuning manual for the Lambretta owner.

Speed has always influenced the younger generation, whether on two or four wheels. For those that chose the scooter, the influence the magazine was having over them was huge. Combined with the actual racing, which had become a big spectator sport, the real age of scooter customisation was beginning to grow. This is where the second major aspect of modification began to evolve at a much faster rate.

The frame was now subject to alteration within the 'special classes' of the racing championships. This would often entail cutting the rear end off the

The scooter scene survived in small pockets all over the country, but it was more prominent up the north

frame right behind the rear seat grille. Though it had been done in the past on scramblers with the old LD models, doing the same to an SX or GP model was something new. With values at their lowest ebb, even a GP that was only a couple of years old could happily sacrifice the rear end of its frame to the racing cause. This would be followed by most, if not all, of the bodywork being removed at the same time. If the leg shields were to remain then they would be significantly narrowed. That's not to say that this is when and where it was first done, but this was the era when the process became mainstream.

Though it would be a few years before the real cutdown revolution started as a scooter fashion, this was where its roots lay – even if it was done for practical reasons initially. With the Lambretta getting faster on the track and owners keen to follow and translate it on to their own machines, it was a significant shift in the way things were going. There was, however, an Achilles heel with it all. The Vespa was still standard and it seemed that for the time being it was going to stay that way. Though many would modify their Lambrettas for performance, there were still many who wouldn't. The reasons are debatable but in all probability it was because mainstream access to tuning was still relatively low and remained localised. Also, because tuning could give reliability issues, who would provide the backup if it went wrong? As the mid-1970s approached, the majority of owners were doing their own maintenance because shops that catered for this need had long since ceased to provide the service. Though it was possible to do the general work yourself, a tuned engine required a totally different approach. Setting up of a carburettor or getting the squish right on a cylinder head needed skill and knowledge to get right. Without the right person to do the job, an owner could be in big trouble.

Most Lambrettas were still standard with the only extra perhaps being a big bore exhaust. Owners still wanted to modify them but painting them a different colour remained the best option. Many were done in the back garden with a tin or two of spray paint. What seemed to be happening was a renaissance of the bolt-on accessory. This trend had never entirely died out as there were still those influenced by the mod style, even though it was a decade old by now. The mainstream had moved on to a large degree but like any fashion it retained its dedicated followers. Perhaps it was Vespa owners who were keeping the tradition alive to some extent as tuning and hacksawing the frame to death wasn't something that was happening with them just yet.

Whatever the reason, accessorising remained an option and began to enjoy a resurgence. Significantly, this showed that diversity was becoming an aspect of scooter ownership and customisation. Not everyone would follow the same path when it came to altering them. Bolting on mirrors and lights might be fine for one person, whereas the next might remove all the bodywork and tune the engine to make it look like a racer. Different avenues of approach began to take shape and this made the scene more interesting. Just as the mods had changed everything on an almost weekly basis, the same seemed to be happening with scooters. It wasn't because owners were following the same fashion again but because they just wanted to be different. There was no other culture like it and though it's been discussed at length and thoroughly researched no one can really give a completely accurate answer as to why this was so. It seems that once bitten by the scooter bug people never lost the urge to constantly alter and change their own machine.

What was more alarming by this time was the end of *Scooter World* magazine. It had been the vital link between scooter owners and the shops who catered for them. With dwindling sales, it could no longer make a profit and sadly closed its doors with the last edition coming out in May 1973. The loss of the magazine signalled perhaps an even greater slowdown in the scooter industry than had been anticipated. There was no halting the decline and with *Scooter World* gone the whole scene or what was left of it went underground. From now on only small pockets of owners would remain and the questions were: where would the scene survive and would it ever come back into the mainstream? If it didn't, then everything scooter-related, including customisation, would eventually be consigned to history.

Chapter Four

The Wilderness Years

The mid-1970s was a difficult time for the scooter scene in the UK. It had been several years since Innocenti had stopped production of the Lambretta and it was now regarded as a machine of the past. Any dealer that was still involved with it only catered for old customers who wanted them servicing or selling off any spares that they were now left with.

There was the odd Serveta Jet 200 coming in from Spain, but it was sporadic. By now the Jet, which was based on the SX 200, was totally outdated so it wasn't easy to sell, certainly if the intention was purely for a mode of transport. Many dealers were still counting their losses on all the old stock and tooling they had leftover from when production finished in 1971. For many, this ran into the thousands and most weren't prepared to invest in something that may not last very long. By now many had moved on to stocking the Japanese motorcycle brands which ruled the industry.

Dealing in second-hand models was all well and good but they could also be easily had out of the local paper at a cheap price. So even that market was difficult for dealers to be involved in. There was no point in buying customers' old machines knowing that you may have to take a loss on them. Many owners who traded their old Lambretta in for a new motorcycle hardly got anything for it. Sometimes customers who had taken machines in to be serviced or repaired never even bothered to pick them up – just leaving them in the back of the shop to gather dust. This crash in value played right into the hands of teenagers. A Lambretta, even in very good condition, could be picked up for just a few pounds and running one was easily affordable.

It was all very fractured in terms of where groups of owners and clubs were based. There is no doubt that the majority of those that remained and were still attracting new members were situated in the north of the country. There were still some clubs in the south, but the scene was very fragmented, to say the least. Why it remained so big in the north has never been fully explained and probably never will be, but it was the towns and cities in that part of the country that really kept scootering alive. The Vespa was still sold and the biggest model, the Rally 200, remained virtually the same as it had been since its revamp in 1973. And that had been based more around the engine than anything else.

With no national magazine to keep owners in touch, the small pockets of clubs that remained had no way of contacting one another and certainly down south they had no real idea what was happening elsewhere. The likes of Rafferty Newman and Arthur Francis were the only real specialists left for the Lambretta, with any other tuning work being taken up by locals on a DIY basis. Both dealers were still producing catalogues and happy to use the mail-order system for anyone wishing to make purchases from them. By this time Arthur Francis himself had handed over the reins of his business to Ray Kemp, who had been with him since starting as an apprentice in the late 1960s. They were the only two left running the shop and Arthur had decided to call it a day. Ray paid a small sum for the entire contents of the shop and the name, eventually renaming it AF Rayspeed Ltd.

By the mid-1970s the only option, if you wanted to buy a new scooter, was the Vespa. Even so, it wouldn't be long before customising it took place

Turning the dying trade around was a huge challenge, but Ray was determined to succeed. He was young and hungry, full of enthusiasm and with his racing background knew he had the knowledge to do the work. Tuning and performance was the only real way forward and he needed to put his ideas to work as soon as possible. The 'S Type' brand which had started there back in the 1960s was a key element of this. If that could continue, then it would provide a solid foundation to build on. That would be Ray's take on the idea from now on. Based in Watford, he soon realised that the majority of his customers were from up north and he found himself dealing with many of them by post. This led to him to relocate to premises near Scarborough in later years – moving closer to his customer base. For now though he would plough on at the existing premises, developing his business idea as best he could.

Where did this leave customisation though? And who was going to move it forward? With the core of scooter owners now in Lancashire and Yorkshire, this was where the answer lay. No one is saying it didn't happen anywhere else, such as in Scunthorpe for instance, but even that was on the Lincolnshire border and just inside the nucleus where things were happening. Many owners were still bolting on extras such as bars and racks which, by this time, were almost being given away by dealers to get rid of them. This was nothing new and neither was painting the bodywork. What was needed now was for someone to take painting that one step further.

Airbrushing images onto a scooter was almost unheard of and the only time that type of

Maca's custom Lambretta labelled Superfly, circa 1977. His painting skills were steadily becoming more in demand thanks to this scooter

The flip flop, or as it was also known Bradford backrest, soon became a point upon which to bolt things to

work ever seemed to emerge was on the side of American vans and motorcycle petrol tanks. It was a niche industry and hadn't reached the world of scooters. Paint technology was light years away from what it is now yet some started to become more daring with their designs and anyone turning up with a different style of paintwork was quickly noticed.

Scooter racing was happily surviving and the organisers were determined to keep it alive. This meant there were plenty of machines that still needed painting, with many displaying names on their side panels and front end. They were definitely still an influence as more and more road-going scooters began to copy this style. Anyone with an artistic nature could easily paint a name on a panel without too much of a problem. Another probable influence was coming from the American muscle car scene that was growing thanks to the likes of Santa Pod raceway. Many of the cars would have names emblazoned down the side. The Lambretta side

Naming a scooter became more popular, possibly influenced by the drag racing and custom car scene that was sweeping through the country at the time

panel was the perfect size to copy this idea with big bold lettering announcing the name of the scooter.

The more people who saw these ideas the more that copied them. There were other designs beginning to creep in too, such as complicated patterns using different colours. This was way ahead of simply painting a panel. A design could be made up of intricate tramlines or lattice patterns that could weave in between two different colours. Owners were starting to become more imaginative as paint began to take over. This new style needed to be displayed and unobstructed. Soon machines with elaborate paintwork were devoid of any racks or bars. What was the point of going to all that work to produce something magnificent and then hiding it all underneath a pile of steelwork? These new creations were simply scooters without too many extras as a different look slowly began to emerge.

The Joker, an early incarnation from Lens scooters, based in Leeds,
as they began to develop their idea of a dealer special. The rear mud flap
was an individual choice but as competition grew so did the flaps
themselves to ridiculous sizes

Early incarnations were made up of murals laid on a panel, often complemented by chrome work. A lot of the chrome was beginning to appear on the engine as well as the forks and hubs. This would make it all stand out and produce what at the time was an eye-catching scooter. Perhaps it was a way of still using chrome but on components of the scooter itself rather than something extra that was bolted on. Rallies were held mainly at the northern coastal resorts of the UK and these became the ideal place for a newly customised scooter to be shown off. Whenever a new scooter was displayed, its influence soon began to rub off – the beginnings of a new revolution that was about to engulf the scootering world. The whole of the scooter scene still had its roots embedded in the mod culture of the 1960s. Even though that scene was long gone, Vespa and Lambretta owners nurtured that original sense of one-upmanship; an intense rivalry to be better than the next person. Unlike in the 1960s, when it had been about the clothes and the look too, now it was the purely about the scooters themselves. Concentrating on just this one thing meant that the competition could accelerate at a much faster pace.

One of the first painters who would rise to prominence was Brendan McNally, more commonly known as Maca. Starting off at home, he soon showed a natural artistic talent when it came to painting scooters. His first real attempt was a Lambretta going by the name of 'Superfly' – an Italian GP with clever block work following the lines of the Bertone styled bodywork. Appearing at rallies and meets, it stood out from the crowd with owners keen to know who the painter was. There weren't too many places where owners could get this style of work done so Maca soon began to get enquiries about it. Realising he could make a go of this as a possible business, he was keen to oblige.

As paint began to take over as the number one customisation art form, dealers also began to see its potential. One of the first was Lens of Shipley, based near Leeds. Already an established Vespa dealership, the company was quick to exploit this new idea. The Rally 200 was still a popular scooter so Lens began to offer them with custom paint jobs. It was nothing too extravagant but even so it attracted customers who wanted their scooter to be different.

As time went by, the firm would continue to take things further with muraled images. These were added to the Vespa's side panels as they were the standout part of the bodywork. Quite often the muraling would include the toolbox door and perhaps the front of the leg shields and the horn casting. The advantage of just doing the side panels and toolbox door meant the whole scooter didn't need to be sent away for painting – just these items – making the job much easier.

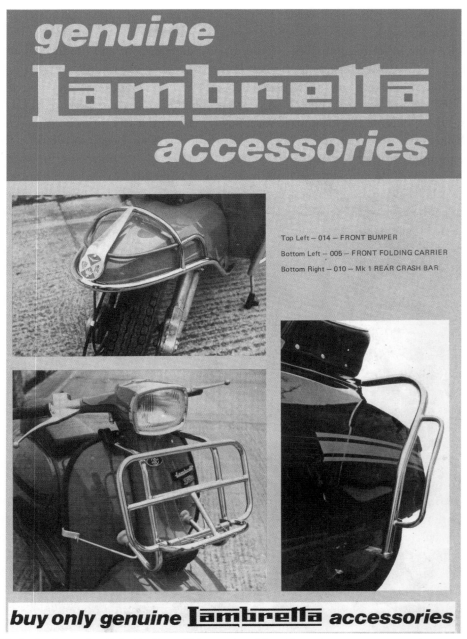

With the launch of the Indian GP in 1978, Two Four Accessories quickly tried to cash in by offering extras on top on the scooter itself

The Lambretta now had so many options when it came to customisation that it was difficult to see what direction it would go in. The big carburettor would be part of it regardless

The Vespa did have parts of its mainframe painted like the Grimstead and Mona specials of the 1960s but this meant it could be off the road for a considerable period of time. A brand-new Vespa with its clean paintwork didn't need anything doing to it. The side panels could be redone but why not enjoy what had come out of the factory for a couple of years before repainting it? In years to come this idea would change, with many being painted from new, but for now it was gradually being introduced into the latest style.

It didn't take long for the film Quadrophenia to make an impact. Here the name is sprayed on the side panels of this Vespa

The popularity of chrome work continued to grow, with more and more components being exposed to this type of treatment. Wheels, hubs and in some cases the front forks. This allowed the running gear to stand out and offset the paintwork. It was more common on the Lambretta simply because those owning a brand-new Vespa might not want to go down this route just after purchasing.

There was another angle too; one that probably originated from the racetrack. Once a Lambretta engine was tuned, a larger carburettor would need to be fitted. In most cases and certainly by this time that would mean one made by Dellorto. In

With the side panels removed, engine tuned and chromed and a Snetterton seat added, a distinct new style was beginning to form

order for it to breathe correctly, a hole would need to be cut out on the left-hand side panel, since otherwise it was too close to the mouth of the carburettor's intake. Originally a small circular hole was cut out in the correct position on the panel to let the air in. But some owners were now cutting a larger area away in a styled shape that followed the contour of the engine, thus exposing the area underneath.

To balance the look, it was also being done on the opposite side panel. Some would take it even further and do away with the side panels completely. The exposed area didn't look that good though, the effect perhaps being similar to that

The Vespa was more subtly introduced to this new look with paint still being the main means of altering its appearance

of removing the bonnet of a car and revealing the engine. This is where chrome came to the rescue and items such as the petrol tank, toolbox or side casing and even the exhaust were transformed. Some began to use copper plating as well – which could complement the paint depending on what colour it was.

Both the Lambretta and the Vespa could have additional chrome in the form of front crash bars or the odd rack. It wasn't a throwback to the mirrors and lights style of the 1960s mods however, even though the odd one or two scooters would have a few fitted. It seemed to be purely based around bars and nothing else. At the back of the frame, there was yet another fashion which seemed to be growing – certainly up in the north of the country: rather than fit a rear rack, which often carried the spare wheel, a sloped back style rack with a small pad was fitted. This was often referred to as the flip flop rack or more commonly the 'Bradford' backrest. It looked stylish and was to become ever-present on both the Lambretta and Vespa. It didn't take long for it to be used as a platform for bolting things on to either.

At the back, many owners would fit a plaque of their scooter club boldly on display to anyone who was following behind. Brake lights began to appear on the outer bars

Artwork was still at its early stage of development but was definitely the way forward as the decade came to a close

and the small square padded area was replaced with something double the size. It was as if the competition was now focused on how different the back of the scooter could be made to look, as opposed to the front which had always been the tradition. Even huge mud flaps, often removed from lorries, would be installed – almost dragging along the floor. On the Vespa they were as wide as the back of the machine but on the much narrower Lambretta they often extended past both sides by some considerable distance.

A new more compact Vespa was launched in 1977 and made its way to the UK a year later. Labelled the P range, it would become available in 125, 150 and 200cc formats – the first and the last aimed at the UK market. It still followed the same pressed steel construction and overall layout but looked far more modern with its squared-off edges. With a powerful reliable engine and competitive price, it was guaranteed to be a winner. Piaggio had put a lot of time and resources into the new model but it has to be remembered that the company was targeting the whole of

The cutdown look developed more out of what was known as the Skelly but would be taken much further over the next few years

the European market, not just the UK. Regardless, it was good news as there was a momentum building up within the scene. Though still underground there seemed to be more and more people getting into scooters and not just in the north either. There were small pockets of clubs forming in other parts of the country as if they were getting ready for something to happen. Piaggio was pushing the Vespa hard in the UK – hardly surprising really because although the P range was good it still needed advertising.

Elsewhere, the Lambretta was attempting a return. Not through Innocenti, as that was long gone, but through Scooters India Limited (SIL). The company had bought the rights to the GP model back in 1971 and now, with it in full

Painted art was still been mixed in with bars and racks but the latter would soon disappear as the paint took centre stage

production, they saw a chance to offer it to the UK again. Some critics said it wasn't as good as the Italian version and there were no revisions or updates. In a way they were right, as it was totally outdated by this time. Quite ironically the importer would be a company called Two Four Accessories, originally set up by Peter Agg who had imported the Lambretta from Innocenti years earlier. Two Four was now under the umbrella of Suzuki GB, which Agg was a major part of.

Finally, the man in control of Two Four was none other than Arthur Francis – who had taken the job on after selling his business to Ray Kemp. It was almost as if they thought the whole Lambretta idea could be resurrected and brought into the mainstream once again. It would soon become apparent that this was not going to be the instant success they thought it would be. Problems with machines both in terms of quality and transportation damage were making things even harder.

Even more problematic was the price, which wasn't cheap by the time the scooters had arrived in the UK. With many good second-hand Innocenti examples available far cheaper and better quality it was much easier for people to buy one of them instead. The only real potential customer base was the younger generation as those wanting general two-wheeled transport had long since moved on from the old outdated Lambretta. Regardless, Two Four continued pushing it in the press as the concession tried to get a foothold in the market. With both Two Four and Piaggio with the P range making a noise in the press, some of the coverage was bound to make an impact.

This still wasn't enough to cause a huge upheaval though and something else was needed. The Reformed LCGB had started laying on rallies once again and this time they were at the bottom half of the country in Southend. This had been going on previously and was the brainchild of Mike Karslake, keeping the Lambretta

**Some now regard the late 1970s look of the Lambretta as its most iconic.
Simplistic by today's standards of customisation but able to make
an impact nonetheless**

name alive. With the LCGB now providing full support the rally began to gain a
bigger profile. This time scooterists from the north would travel down to join in,
pushing everyone together. Now there were custom scooters on show to a new
audience who were keen to follow this exciting trend.

By now there was a heightened atmosphere that something big was about to
happen. Even the big music magazines were tipping the next fashion to be a mod
revival. Punk was on its way out and exciting new wave bands were on the rise.
Though not directly connected to the scooter, everything that was happening in
1978 from the new Vespa and Lambretta to the music had a direct link. That's
when the final part of the jigsaw fell into place. The Who was by this time a world-
renowned band and they had decided to produce a film based around their 1974
album Quadrophenia. The tale of a young mod from London growing up in the

Dellorto Sprint – a forerunner to one of the most famous custom Lambrettas ever built

In the main scooters were still fairly plain in 1979 but all that was about to change in the following decade

1960s was bound to stir up enthusiasm, not so much from those that were there at the time but the new young generation of teenagers waiting to join in the next big thing.

Thought it wouldn't be released until 1979, many scooter owners who by chance had seen the advert for extras were going to be part of it. There was no doubt as to whether the film was going to be as good as anticipated – it would have a huge impact whatever the case. At the centre of the whole thing was the scooter and there was a good possibly that this climactic coming together of different driving forces could push ownership to new heights not seen since the 1960s. With customisation starting to build, it too had the potential to reach new levels as thousands joined in. What shape or direction it would go in was anyone's guess, but one thing was guaranteed – it would be exciting times ahead.

Chapter Five

Anything Goes

Quadrophenia made a bigger impact on the scooter scene than anything else had since the 1960s. The film has been well documented over the years and almost anyone who has owned a scooter since its release in 1979 will have been influenced by it. There is no need to go into too much detail other than to note that it was the spark which ignited the huge mod revival that ensued across the nation that year.

Not every single teenager joined in, but a huge majority of them did. The scooter was an integral part of this movement and ownership of both the Vespa and Lambretta increased dramatically. There was a far bigger consequence in that people from all over the country became engaged. No longer was it a fashion predominately set in the north of the country. From the southern counties all the way up to Scotland, a new and exciting scooter revolution had begun.

Just like in the past, the appearance of the scooters themselves changed – those living out the mod dream yet again bolted mirrors and lights on to their scooters. It must be remembered that those who had kept the underground scene going all this time were by now slightly older than those just starting out. They had already been through this phase and to them the scooter was more important than the quick-fire new mod fashion that had exploded out of nothing.

They would now be responsible for the real custom look of scooters. The change had been under way even before Quadrophenia was released, so why should they in effect go backwards by doing what was deemed fashionable? If anything, many of the older owners tried to distance themselves from what was going on. Perhaps they were feeling a bit more grown-up and past this phase in their lives.

With thousands of new scooter owners and a vibrant scene beginning to grow, the revival was in full swing. But like any teenage fashion it didn't last long. By the summer of 1980 it was in decline, just as quickly as it had started. Some would now move on to whatever trend was next, dumping their whole attire in the process – including their scooter. Many more had been bitten by the scooter bug however, and though they too would get out of the mod revival their scooter would remain in their possession. It was a new dawn within a scene that now consisted of the

Time Trouble and Money, built at the beginning of the 1980s, is regarded as one of the most important custom Lambrettas ever built

staunch supporters from the lean times of the 1970s and the new influx who were leftover from the revival. It was an ideal mix as it would provide the scene with some sort of stability. The older owners would keep it going regardless of how many new ones dropped out.

As the new decade got under way, scooter ownership across the country was continuing to grow as other teenagers got into the scene. Some were those who had perhaps been slightly too young to get involved in the revival but were influenced by their friends who had. All that mattered now was scooters and though the 1980s would be the decade of the 'scooter boy', not everyone was dictated to by the fashion.

Even in later years when there would be other revivals – such as the one brought about by the 'Britpop' era – it was the scooter that always remained. What the

In its second incarnation a few years later. It remains in this condition to this day

By now Ray Kemp had firmly established the S Type brand and his creations were heavily in demand

Eternal Warrior used a clever mix of painted murals and chrome

Simplistic lines and the exposure of a reverse cone exhaust gave a personal touch for those doing their own customisation

1979 revival and Quadrophenia had done was lay down the perfect platform for the custom scooter to show its real potential. With thousands of owners, many of whom who wanted their scooter to be the best, it was like the perfect storm.

For this to succeed there needed to be several key links in the chain. Shops that could cater for the needs of the owners were essential; not just supplying them with scooters and parts but with the specialist services that were needed too. Painters, fabricators, chrome plating businesses and tuners just for a start. Then there were the rallies that would now grow to almost epic proportions; these were required not just to keep the scooter scene going but to provide a setting where the scooters could be displayed. There would be a customs show at each rally with prizes given in several categories. This would eventually lead to the start

The legendary Armando's dealer special that thrust the P range Vespa into the spotlight and is still sold now

of properly organised custom shows. Finally, there were magazines that would link everything together – advertising where events and rallies were being held, providing a platform where dealers could advertise and, most importantly, ensuring there was a regular and widely available showcase for custom scooters through articles and images.

None of this would happen overnight but as soon as there is a profit to be made it doesn't take long. Thousands of owners were ready to spend huge sums of cash on their pride and joy and entrepreneurs saw a opening. Many of the tuners and scooter builders working in their garages now took the opportunity to set up a shop and make it a steady full-time business. It was a similar situation with the rallies. When there were thousands in attendance there was a lot of money to be made if you got it right. Though there would be no national magazine

Talk o'th North a forerunner to the big explosion in full custom scooters that was about to happen

Muraled side panels now began to get more and more extensive, soon covering other areas of the bodywork

Italian Stallion set a new benchmark that others would have to follow. It had just about everything possible including engraving of certain components

With only the side panels and front end painted, the Vespa could easily be transformed into something special

for a while, a few began to see the possibility of making an independent one pay. Once all these things fell into place, the scene was only going to go one way and it did.

A custom scooter was now starting to be made up of three fundamental areas: the paint, the engine and the chrome work, with the first two being essential. No scooter that was painted could be without a tuned engine – it was almost as if something was missing if you left either out. Engine tuners were setting up shops all over the country to cater for both the Vespa and Lambretta.

It was slightly easier for the Vespa because it was still in production. Companies such as Polini were making aftermarket cylinders which in theory could just be bolted on. For the Lambretta it was different, as a tuner would be required to work on the original cylinder. Though there was plenty of power to be had out of them it still required skill and knowledge to get it exactly right. People such as Dave Webster, Norrie Kerr and the Frankland brothers who set up Taffspeed were just a few of those who would go on to have successful scooter tuning businesses.

Competition among owners would only intensify. If someone had a tuned engine then others would want one more powerful. And the tuner keen to earn his money would do his best to oblige the customer. It was a constant cycle and the best tuners were soon in demand. If something was seen to be different and to improve performance then everyone wanted one fitted to their engine. For those with the real knowledge and the wherewithal to get such things made it could be a big earner. Even the Vespa could be tuned further than just bolting on a kit and these scooters too would see the fitting of items that made them faster. Not everyone got it right and some components, if anything, hampered the engine and

The Lambretta GP with its huge flat surfaces was a painter's dream

Dazzle in its second incarnation and quite rightly the most influential custom scooter ever built

**Mytho Poeikon made its debut at a similar time and became
the standard that all Vespa owners would look up to**

made no improvement whatsoever. They were soon found out and the item would stop selling very quickly. During the 1980s there would be hundreds of items that would supposedly make a scooter faster – and many of them soon lay discarded on the floor of owners' garages.

The biggest tuning product and most lucrative if it worked was the expansion chamber. For both the Vespa and Lambretta it was the quickest way of improving performance. For the owner simply the sound, which was far louder than its standard counterpart, was all that mattered. Even if the scooter didn't go quicker, for many the sound made them think that they actually were. Then there was the look which, to some, was more important than the performance itself.

A great big expansion pipe sticking out the side, perhaps with a chrome tailpipe, looked good and it seemed that's what mattered most. Similarly, the carburettor was quite often just bolted on regardless of what the set up needed to be. With the Lambretta being piston ported, quite often more fuel was spat back out than went into the engine. Fuel efficiency was drastically reduced and given the scooter's

Sign of the Snake became the top custom scooter of 1986 and is still owned by its original builder Mick Howard

Two examples of how the Lambretta Series I and II could be stunningly altered

small tank, range consequently suffered. It didn't seem to bother owners though as the induction roar compensated for these newfound problems. Tuning was a way of not only impressing but seemingly having a sort of one-upmanship over the next owner – even if the set up was all wrong as a result. In the past it was mirrors and lights that made a scooter different, but now it was expansion pipes and carburettors instead.

The paintwork also began to change as the technology of how it was laid down began to improve greatly. All it had been, up to now, was different colours which looked good but didn't really make the scooter individual. Though there had been a few muraled examples, they weren't exactly mainstream at this time. Yet as more skilled airbrush artists arrived on the scene this was all going to change.

There was so much more potential than just painting a picture on the side panel, which was all that was really happening. With the talent out there to cover the entire bodywork of a scooter with lots of different images it now needed the imagination

Even though it was ridiculed at the time, the Jet 200 soon became popular as a custom scooter

of the owner to make it happen. All of a sudden, a scooter could be wholly based around a specific theme such as a band or a film, perhaps someone's hero. This was a totally different concept and the more vivid the owner's imagination the bigger the prize would be. Painters with the expertise were more than happy to take such a task on. They knew that if they got it right then there was bound to be more work as the competition intensified. It was becoming a joint collaboration between the owner, with the vision of how they wanted the scooter to look, and the painter who could make that vision a reality.

The Lambretta was a painter's dream – certainly when it came to the GP. Its huge flat-sided panels were the ideal blank canvas on which to lay down an artistic masterpiece. Also, with the bodywork easily removable, each piece was far easier to work on. The Vespa was much more difficult with a lot of the mainframe at awkward angles and being so big it was difficult to manoeuvre. There were plenty of admirers of the Vespa and no painter was going to turn them down just because they were far more cumbersome and difficult to navigate around. The schemes and designs just needed more thinking out in the first place to get them right.

For now, the chrome work would remain on the major running gear and engine components – continuing the trend as it had started a few years earlier. Of course, there would be bodywork components such as the headset top, front mudguard and horn casting included. The problem was, if a scooter had a theme airbrushed on to it then these parts were painted rather than chromed. It was possible to mix the two styles but this would cause a fragmented scheme if it was not thought out correctly.

The Vespa was also beginning to see a lot more chrome work done and just like the Lambretta there were plenty of components from which to choose.

Three examples of how plain base coats could be mixed with different paint applications to create a unique effect

A new style that was beginning to creep in was with the engine – the cowlings and various engine covers were now being chromed. There was a problem with displaying it all though since most of it was ordinarily hidden from view. The side panel would need removing and leaving just the one on the left-hand side looked rather odd. If both were removed then it would give a rather deep flat strange look.

Removing the panels on a Lambretta looked good but with the Vespa, it simply didn't work. The solution was to cut out a half-moon shape on the right-hand side panel around the contour of its top section. With a rubber beading placed around its edge, this exposed the engine and allowed the chrome work to be in full view. If done correctly it looked professional and proved even a new style PX Vespa could have its bodywork cut out. Owners didn't seem bothered that their machine was almost new and being treated in this way. It was as though in the pursuit of the perfect look anything could be done to get it right – regardless of the consequences. This also showed a levelling out between the two different makes of scooter. Whichever one you owned it was now viable to alter it in whatever way you wished. It was almost as though the shackles were finally off. The result of all this was that scooter customisation was about to enter its golden era with literally thousands of examples ready to be unleashed.

More and more themes started to be based around Northern Soul tunes and singers

With a huge range of accessories offered for the Vespa they began to become part of the artwork

Despite more and more people joining in, it would still require a few at the top to lead the way; the ones who were the most creative with their ideas and could raise the bar that bit higher. This, in turn, would make those following raise their game to beat them. With custom shows at rallies becoming more and more popular the competition stepped up a gear. Rallies were getting bigger by the year so the shows held there were the ideal place to reveal owners' latest creations. In 1983 a new custom scooter called Italian Stallion was taking the scene by storm. It belonged to Martyn Scully and was born out of his first custom scooter built in the late 1970s, East Coast Connection. Martyn was from Barnsley in South Yorkshire and a staunch Lambretta enthusiast. His scooter's new incarnation was something totally different and there is no doubt that it would become one of the scooters that raised customisation to the next level.

It was built around an Italian GP 200 and based on the theme of the film Rocky III. It had everything a custom scooter owner at the time could have dreamed of. The paint was by Maca, who now had an established paint business called Down Town Custom also based in Yorkshire. It was made up of a set of murals around the body with the name in bold lettering across the side panels. The engine was tuned to the highest specification available. Everything that wasn't painted was chromed and the side panels were elegantly cut out to show it all off. On the top was a Snetterton seat that had been specially covered and was different to anything else available. The attention to detail was its crowning glory; cables were covered with neat shrouds, the battery was encased in a purpose-made box and all the bolts and fasteners were chromed.

There was one final touch – one that had never been seen before. Certain items such as the rear light unit, air scoop and most prominently the side casing were engraved. The process was done by stripping them to bare metal, engraving them, and then finished them off with chroming. It wasn't excessive or over the top but complemented the overall look perfectly. It showed thinking totally outside of the box and served as a warning to those building new scooters that they needed to step things up if they wanted to beat it. At shows, Italian Stallion defeated everything else hands down. Not so much because it had something new, like engraving, but because the whole thing was as close to perfection as you could get. Producing something better would require a truly sensational piece of work.

Scooter ownership was still growing and so were the businesses that catered for those owners. Whatever part of the industry a shop was involved with, this was the time to make money. Many new components began to make their way on to the market – even for the Lambretta. It was much harder to do this compared to the Vespa because an individual would have to stump the money up for the tooling rather than a large company. Producing parts or accessories for a scooter that wasn't manufactured anymore could be regarded as a gamble. For the time being it was a safe one though, since the market was strong but how long would it last for? The more products that became available the easier it was to build or alter a scooter and this in itself gave owners new ideas of what to do.

With Italian Stallion setting a new standard, not long after another scooter made its debut entitled Dazzle. This shocked the whole scooter scene to its core. It was a huge step up from what had previously been seen. Painted in blue and purple, it featured several murals dedicated to the band Siouxsie and the Banshees. Almost every other component that wasn't painted was chromed and on top of that the engraving covering a considerable surface area of the whole machine. Items such as the tanks and cowlings, the wheels and forks, even the exhaust were all subject to the same treatment. Its owner was Jeremy Howlett and his attention detail and the ethic that everything must be right was clear to see in what he had created.

Though Dazzle was streets ahead it didn't seem to quite get the recognition or attention it deserved. Jeremy, always trying to improve on things, decided to pull it apart and get it done all over again. He kept the same name and theme but this time the base colour was green. Overhauling what was already a new custom

**Throughout the decade the custom show became a major part of the
scootering calendar, creating huge competition among owners**

scooter seemed wasteful to some and at the time there was criticism over this. He
wanted everything to be correct though, and if it wasn't then wholesale changes
were needed. Perhaps it was a problem created by Jeremy himself in the pursuit of
perfection. Soon all the talk died down and regardless he carried on – thankfully,
as many regarded the green reincarnation of Dazzle the best custom scooter ever
built.

Jeremy would go on to build several other custom scooters, each seemingly
better than the previous one, and with some amazing engineering and artistic work
to complement them. Even though they were another level up from Dazzle, that
was definitely the scooter that set the standard followed to this day. It was ground-
breaking in many ways and who knows what direction the custom scene would
have taken without Jeremy's input. Those craftsmen whose services he used at
the time became prominent, with everyone wanting the best. Dave Webster from
Midland Scooter Centre tuned the engine. He was already very popular among
Lambretta owners but now became regarded as the must-have tuner if you were

All That Jazz, the Lambretta that allegedly ignited the street racer scene

going to build the best custom Lambretta. Likewise Paul Karslake, who painted Dazzle, became heavily in demand. Don Blocksidge, who did the engraving, came to the public's attention working on many scooters since then – primarily because of Dazzle.

With the competition cranked up a gear by Dazzle, those wanting to build a full-blown custom scooter would have to go one step further. Thankfully this was begging to spill over into the territory of Vespa owners. It didn't matter if a P range was a few years old or brand new. Now they too were being subject to the complete range of ideas seen on Dazzle. Engraving on a new Vespa or even more radical alterations proved there were no rules or boundaries on what was allowed. As the number of new custom scooters appearing changed from a trickle to a flow it became increasingly hard to keep up with the competition. Newly completed examples were appearing on an almost daily basis, each incorporating new and different ideas. Sometimes if the build was slow the end product would almost look a bit dated by the time it was shown to the public – such was the accelerated rate of development.

Though the full-blown custom scooter was a major part of the scene, other styles were now becoming firmly established. This would require a different

The AF Genesis street racer based around the idea of the TS1 entering a production class in the British scooter racing championships

type of thinking but there is no doubt that the 1980s was the decade when almost anything seemed possible when it came to the scooter. Cutdowns had been around for years and were prolific on the racetrack, where they first really came to light. Now they were fashionable on the road too and it wasn't just with Lambrettas either. Vespa owners were also beginning to follow this emerging fashion. The PX by this time had been in production for a few years so cheaper second-hand models were becoming available. Cutting one down didn't seem such a bad thing to do, even though it would lower the resale value of it in the future.

Getting the right look with the Vespa when cutting it down wasn't as easy as doing it with the Lambretta. For the Lambretta, it was simple and straightforward. You just sawed off the back end behind the rear frame grille and removed all the

The water-cooled GP built by Mark Broadhurst. This idea had been championed back in the 1970s but would become more popular after the introduction of the TS1

bodywork by unbolting it. If you wanted to cut down the leg shields then that was an easy enough procedure to carry out. If you decided to revert back, then all you had to do was get another pair and bolt them on.

The Vespa did not allow this flexibility because its monocoque frame meant once something was removed it couldn't be put back on. The bigger problem was at the back, with the deep narrow sides behind the panels. Though a lot of this would want removing it couldn't be too excessive because this was the area that housed the petrol tank. It would take careful consideration and skill as there were a lot of edges and contours to work around. At the front, the leg shields didn't want to be too narrow – otherwise the squared-off horn casting would look odd. Also, the floor still needed to have enough area left around where the brake pedal was located.

When it was done right, the Vespa cutdown could look good; but when too much of the bodywork was removed it looked a bit odd and flimsy. The Lambretta on the other hand suited this look perfectly with its steel tube frame. With or without leg shields fitted, however much the scooter was narrowed didn't really matter. The look was also helped by the double-sided forks compared to the single side type of the Vespa which looked strange when exposed.

At the back of the Lambretta, the standard dual seat was removed as it now looked totally out of place. The squared-off Snetterton seat with its low frame was ideally suited as a replacement. It was the same with the Vespa also and dealers were now coming up with their own low-level seat designs which were popular with those following this type of style. Another modification which began to emerge was the fitting of a petrol tank in the gap between the headset and the mainframe shell. It was most popular on the Lambretta and required a simple modification of welding a tube on the gap in the mainframe to which a tank was mounted. It almost gave a motorcycle chopper kind of look – but it worked.

This type of modification was an integral part of another style that was now making waves through the scene: the full-blown chopper. Again, this was a style that dated back to the late 60s early 70s when it appeared on old LD models. Though it was possible with a Vespa, and some did try, it was suited more to the Lambretta – purely because of its frame dimensions and layout. A chopper conversion would start off with just the actual frame tube minus all the struts and the frame top shell. Because the forks would be extended, in some cases considerably, this would require the fork stem to be raked further back. Failure to do this would make the handlebars almost unreachable and leave the rider sitting at an awkward angle. Once the rake was correct a cross member could be put in for the petrol tank. The seat would be positioned on the curve of the frame where the petrol tank originally sat.

This type of customising really required some thought since, in theory, a totally different machine was being created out of an old one. A full-bodied Lambretta customisation might have new paint and some different extras made or fitted but with a chopper, apart from the engine, everything else was a one-off. The more popular the style got, the more radical the choppers became. Soon there was huge competition on the scene and because the scooters were all unique the creations became ever more outrageous.

The explosion in customisation only made the scene even stronger and these new scooter styles were welcomed with open arms. It showed just how diverse the scene could be and though not everyone would like every style that didn't seem to matter and everything was accepted.

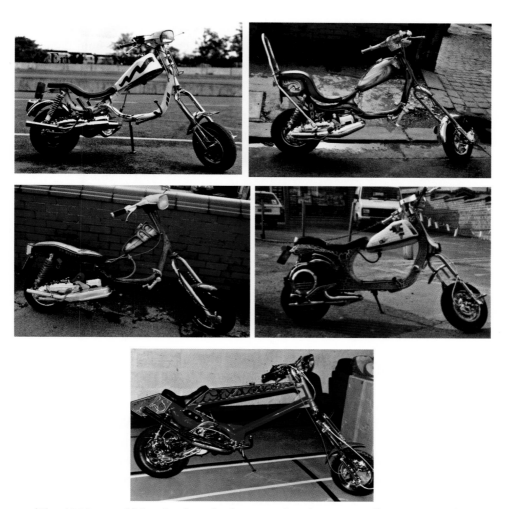

The 1980s would be the decade that saw the chopper really arrive on the custom scene. From those that were modified frames to the downright radical. All unique in their own way

As the decade moved on, custom shows had long since become an integral part of scooter rallies. Many clubs and organisations began to hold their own shows which in turn created even more interest. These became big events in their own rights, and some gained a reputation as the place where new machines would be unveiled for the first time. It was the perfect place to do so in front of a big crowd.

Scooters such as Dazzle and Mytho Poeikon – one of the top Vespas at the time – would rule the circuit for a while. Soon other machines would take their place, but this would only encourage the owners of the best scooters to upgrade them or build another one that was even better in an attempt to regain their crown. There were more and more shows starting up all over the country but there were plenty of entrants to fill the halls and big attendances were almost guaranteed. All of these factors meant that the custom scene remained strong for several years and looked to have a bright future.

After a time though, people did start to ask whether everything had now been done when it came to modifying and customising the scooter. Many things had been tried in a relatively short period of time. Perhaps it had got to saturation point or at least a place where people needed to take a breather before the next style emerged. There were plenty of owners still coming out with different themes and ideas though, so why worry about it? With a much bigger choice of painters and tuners now offering their services, there were bound to be more scooters built. Though many of the practices had been seen time and time again, such as engraving, this didn't mean to say that the scooters were all the same. There were those constantly looking to come up with a different style and possibly the answer lay back with one of the places where it had first started – the racetrack.

Towards the end of the 1980s scooter racing was at its peak in the UK – with more licence holders than ever before. Many of the racers were beginning to copy paint schemes from the motorcycle world. At that time, it was dominated by tobacco sponsorship with some great colour combinations. With sponsors' logos appearing all over the fairings they certainly stood out. Tuning was as big as ever thanks to the launch of the T5 for the Vespa and the TS1 kit for the Lambretta. A tuned engine had been a standard requirement of the custom scooter for some time but with this area experiencing rapid growth, the focus began to switch to building a scooter purely based around the engine itself.

During this period a scooter was featured on the back page on an edition of *Scooterist Scene* magazine called All That Jazz. It was painted in white with green overlay and it had a tuned engine to match. Within the text lay a claim that the street racer had arrived – which to some extent was true. It wasn't so much that this one was the first, there had been others before it, but this was a custom scooter that was purely based around the race look. Scooters such as the AF 'S Type' Lambretta had been around a long time and by now had legendary status. AF Rayspeed could only produce so many – so there were never going to be hundreds of them. The company had launched its own version of a TS1 'Genesis' special.

The cutdown took on many different guises to achieve the same end result

It was originally intended to be sold so that a production class could be based around it, forming a new category in scooter racing. That didn't get off the ground, however, despite its stunning looks. The same could be said of the 'Armando's special' Vespa which was based around a similar style. All this went a long way to proving the street racer concept was still in its infancy.

It was a slow build-up with other shops beginning to create their own dealer specials too. Building a full-blown custom scooter required several different specialists and took a long time to sort – something that a shop on its own couldn't do. A street racer was different, especially for those that were good engine tuners to boot. Not only could they produce an eye-catching scooter but it would advertise their tuning skills too by way of its engine. As more and more of these began to appear, the bigger the street racer scene started to become. Because they were built around performance many of them had the latest technology available anywhere in the scooter world fitted.

As the Lambretta was made to go faster it needed more stopping power. Improved versions of the hydraulic disc brake which had been around since the mid-1970s started to appear. And items such as the clutch would need upgrading to cope with the extra power that was being produced. A great many new developments were happening all the time, many of them coming straight off the race track. Those who could offer new ideas that actually worked would soon end up selling their products in sizable quantities to eager customers who wanted the latest must-have thing on their scooter. Though the T5 Vespa was already in a tuned state from the factory, that didn't stop tuners from trying to get even more out of them. This involved not only conversion kits but a whole host of expansion pipes that were soon on the market. The T5 had taken the scooter world by storm and it quickly became the Vespa rider's street racer. Machines were being painted and the engines tuned the moment they were run in. In some cases, scooters would get a full-blown custom makeover before they had even turned a wheel.

As the decade came to an end the street racer concept was in full swing and it gave a new and refreshing concept to the custom scene. The big benefit was to the shows themselves which now had more entrants and could offer those attending even more different perspectives to look at. If you wanted murals and elaborate artwork, it was on show. If you wanted striking but simple paint jobs and a scooter free from too much chrome and engraving, that was now available also. Individualism, when it came to the scooter, was as popular as ever and the scene as whole was very healthy. Whether or not this was the peak period for custom scooters being built is debatable, but it certainly was one of the strongest periods. A lot of it came down to all the new styles that were still relatively new and fresh. As time moved on, the same ideas being repeated over and over perhaps would become less interesting to the masses. Customisation of scooters was never going to stop but it might not be on such a grand scale in the future.

Chapter Six

Levelling Off

The custom scene of the 1980s was so frenetic there was virtually no time to catch your breath. It was a decade where seemingly anything with the scooter was possible and the scooters created during that time would be a hard act to follow. Countless Lambrettas and Vespas had been altered and changed way beyond anyone's imagination. Some were so modified that they could never be put back to how they once were. Why would they be reverted though? Many of these creations were masterpieces and it would seem a shame to get rid of them.

There was a problem beginning to emerge however, with many custom scooter owners following a similar path. For various reasons they now wanted to sell their machines. It could be simply that they just wanted to move on or that funds needed to be raised to build another one. Though most that came up for sale were in good if not perfect condition, their creators could never get the money back that had been put into them in the first place.

Some of the full-blown custom scooters had been on the receiving end of big paint jobs and featured large areas of costly engraving. And there was a stigma attached to buying a custom scooter that someone else had created. The new owner would be made well aware of this – which would lead them to change the scooter's looks, perhaps with alterations to the paint.

This wasn't an easy thing to do and there was the question of just how much would need changing before the new owner was happy that they had put their mark on it. This would add more cost too, meaning the new owner would want to get it done as cheaply as possible.

All this meant that some custom scooters were losing value and by a considerable margin. They could also be advertised for quite a while before someone was prepared to buy them. In all honesty, the original owners didn't worry too much that they couldn't recoup all the money they had put into the scooter. Just the satisfaction alone in what they had created was enough recognition.

It was about creating something special – not making money out of the project. Knowing that you would probably lose out financially if you built a custom scooter

The AF race team had their machines painted by DTC which would become an iconic and much-copied scheme

didn't seem to deter people and many new ones were still being built or commissioned.

There was a general and noticeable slowdown compared to a few years earlier. It wasn't just in custom scooters but the whole scooter scene in general was in a bit of a lull. This was hardly surprising as some had been into it for a long time and were older now – perhaps with a family to support and a mortgage to pay. Scooters were being built at a much slower rate. Also, the dynamic of what was in vogue had changed. Muraled scooters on themes were still being done but to a much lesser extent. The street racer was now beginning to take centre stage.

Why this should have become the case remains unclear but perhaps people were getting bored of the same old thing. Themes were always original and it was down to each owner's imagination what the final result would be. Perhaps it was that the techniques used were becoming boring. Chrome was getting a bit old hat and long in the tooth. After all, there was only so many times you could look at some plated engine parts and be amazed. Along with that went engraving; people were starting to question whether the process was ethically right, certainly when referring to the Lambretta. It was over 20 years since Innocenti had finished production and certain parts were starting to become rare and hard to find. Once items such as a side case or headset gear and switch housings had been engraved, they were scrap and unusable on anything else. As preserving the Lambretta slowly began to happen practices like this were seen by some as blasphemous.

Paint ideas were also begging to change as the street racer look didn't really work with the mural. Now it was race logos and anything to do with the performance that was the latest craze. That's probably why engraving and chrome were also suddenly out of fashion as they didn't fit in with the street racer look either. There would always be the custom purist who thought different meaning though there was a shift there was now more to see at shows or in magazine features. With the tuning market still strong thanks to the TS1 for the Lambretta and the T5 Vespa, the street racer was here to stay even if it was pushing a few people's noses out of joint.

As the 1990s moved on the lull in the scooter scene was beginning to take its toll. Some dealers who had enjoyed the boom in the 1980s were now starting to doubt the industry. Some even quit altogether, worried that if they didn't they would get into debt as they carried on. Just as it seemed things could only get worse there was a reversal of fortunes. This was being fuelled by the new 'Britpop' culture which was supposedly influencing a new breed of mods. It was a much more watered-down affair than before and influencing it somewhat was the launch of a Lambretta clothing range. This was only licenced use of the name, but it shoved the iconic brand back in the limelight once again.

Also painted by DTC one of the most popular examples at the time was this one based on the colours of the Williams Honda Formula 1 team

One of the Jade Scooters dealer specials which features the three band diagonal stipe across the side panels, cleverly incorporating the number block

Helping the cause was an influx of scooters now being imported from Italy. With borders having come down a few years previously, as Europe attempted to be one, it was far easier to export them to the UK. So easy in fact that people were literally going over to Italy, filling up a van with both Vespas and Lambrettas then driving back to the UK almost on a weekly basis. Scooters were still redundant to a large extent in Italy – even though interest had picked up with the country's national Lambretta club being re-formed in 1988. It was good that interest had been rekindled but it would take time for things to really take off over there. With so many Lambrettas still left over from the past there were plenty to go around. The extra bonus was their price. Good running

The T5 dominated the street racer look when it came to the Vespa

The Vespa PX was still a popular choice for customisation at the beginning of the 1990s but faded somewhat by the end of that decade

examples that were untampered with cost only a few hundred pounds – even including the cost of getting them to the UK.

It couldn't have come at a better time as the resurgence in the scene began to build once again. It had always been a wave-like effect, with popularity growing for a few years before fashions changed – only for interest to rise again at a later date. It was a pattern that had been around since the 1960s and that's how it would always continue. This resurgence was big though and was aided and abetted by the return of some of those who had been around in the late 1970s early 1980s. They were older, their children had grown up and their mortgages were well on the way to being paid off. This suddenly left them with a disposable income and a desire to relive their youth through the scooter.

As demand soared once more, prices began to rise and this gave a timely boost to dealers. Many new shops were beginning to sprout up with the thought of making a fast buck. All of this helped the custom scene gather pace again. For a while things became a bit confused as the mod look with mirrors and lights once again made a brief appearance. There was also a resurgence in the original look as some scooters were restored back to factory specification. Though this fashion might have been uninspiring to those who liked the custom scooter, it slowly started to add a new dimension. Owners were now starting to fit original accessories and as usual the competition between them began to grow. This movement gained such a following that it now became included at custom shows and had its own classes.

A well-prepared Group 3 race Lambretta that had many attributes which would be replicated on road-going street racers

Race machines were becoming more colourful and the schemes became a direct influence

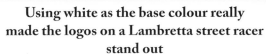

Using white as the base colour really made the logos on a Lambretta street racer stand out

As the competition and intensity grew so did the outlandish colours and schemes

As long as it swelled the attendance though, that was all that mattered. There was a lot on offer at custom shows during this period – with a bigger choice to look at, influencing others to join in.

The street racer was still leading the way and this was getting help from dealers. People such a Mark Broadhurst were starting to produce their own tuning products for the Lambretta. It no longer needed big manufacturers to get involved – an individual could take on the same risk because the market was strong enough to make it financially viable. The ease with which a tuned engine could be built encouraged builders to turn ideas and concepts previously regarded as outlandish or unrealistic into a reality. This led to the introduction of water-cooled cylinders, six-plate clutches and so on, all based around the goal of achieving greater power and performance.

The street racer was being taken to a new level. Those building them wanted the most powerful engine and trick parts to make their creation better than anyone else's. And now they had the tools to do exactly that. Scooter racing had reached its peak in the UK and racers and tuners were developing some great ideas. Those with a business knew that if they could market an innovation already proven on the track then it could be a good seller. This was quite often showcased by way of a new dealer special – a race-prepared scooter with all the latest items that was road legal. Matching the paintwork to the performance soon made customers flock in.

Items such as outboard disc brakes, upgraded suspension and many other parts intended to improve performance appeared on the market. As had been the case over the preceding decades, there were still plenty of ideas claiming to be good that were more of a gimmick or gave no benefit whatsoever. They soon got binned off but those dealers who got it right only grew their business even more. Owners soon started to cherry-pick the best items and use the best tuners to create what in their mind was the ultimate street racer.

Another take on the three-band layout that is still widely used today

Painters were also drafted in to exclusively finish these creations off. Many of them were used to painting murals and elaborate designs but now found themselves doing more logos instead. It was a way of making a living though and they did whatever the customer wanted in order to pay the bills. A lot of the time it would be the painter who was now responsible for coming up with the scheme for the scooter.

A customer might request specific logos and a certain race number on the side panels, but it was the painter who was responsible for making it look good. A lot of it was still being influenced by race cars and bikes. After all, companies like Ferrari spent millions getting the look right for the Formula 1 audience and it was far easier to just reinterpret what they were doing or simply reuse their colour palette. The skill was getting the look right without the design seeming too complicated or cluttered. Just because there was a lot of space on the Lambretta bodywork, it didn't necessarily have to be swamped with logos.

The custom shows now had dedicated classes for full-blown custom scooters, street racers, standards, choppers, engineering, even best oddity for oddball creations. With the scene getting stronger, dealers were also starting to have bigger stalls at events. The big customs shows were now a huge gathering of what was available within the industry, catering for all needs. The scooters were the central attraction. It was welcome news after the downturn at the beginning of the decade and proved that the scene was strong and could survive even in the leanest of times. That alone was enough to guarantee new creations would keep coming because the competition was still there. No one was sure what the next fashion would entail or what would be the most popular style of custom scooter. There would always be room for whatever anyone wanted to build – which was most important.

**Starting in the late 1980s but taking hold in the 1990s was the
Sixties street racer look**

The street racer just went from strength to strength as the manufacturers' efforts began to gather pace. The news that more cylinder kits were in the pipeline and that they would be faster was music to owners' ears. Also starting to creep in was the classic street racer which was championed by the Lambretta. Many were based around the old Arthur Francis 'S Type' and 'Supertune' schemes but others were unique just using old technology. The odd one or two had first been done in the late 1980s but this idea was becoming more popular and added another angle to the idea. Some were even using modern-day engines and technology but mixing it with old-style paint schemes. It proved that no matter what style of scooter it was and how far the idea had been taken, if you thought long and hard enough there was still further room for development.

The magazines were also happy to feature just about any creation going. Not only did it give variety for the reader but also ideas for those ready to build their

Babe Ruth was a mix of the custom and street racer look. It lacked chrome and engraving but still carried extensive murals

In the quest to come up with something different the scooter could take on a totally different look. It showed that customising had no boundaries

The 1990s was also the decade where it had gone full circle and restoring scooters back to their former glory was accepted

next scooter. No matter what it is in life, we all look at what has been created before as an influence — whether it's music, fashion or custom scooters it's all the same.

Sometimes there would be blatant copies of ideas and those who thought theirs had been ripped off often vented their anger. It should have been taken as a compliment that someone thought the idea was good enough to copy in the first place. The fierce competition that has always been present in the custom scene would not allow that though. Copying wasn't too prevalent, and most looked at it simply as 'idea borrowing'.

The engineering side was where this was most common and the cutdown or chopper was the most exploited concept. There were only certain ways in which either make could be engineered into a chopper so it was inevitable that the same methods would be used again and again. It was down to the paint style or theme to make the real difference. This wasn't as easy as it sounded because most of the bodywork would have been removed and there wasn't much left to paint. Full-blown custom scooters were slightly different in that way, but many were based around the same theme – such as a popular band for example. It was down to the painter to give it individuality and make it stand out compared to the next one and those that were the most skilled were given that the responsibility. Some even painted the same theme several times, each time a little differently.

As the century came to an end there was a noticeable shift happening towards the Lambretta. It had always had the upper hand due to its bigger flatter surface

The NSRA stand at the NEC showed all styles of customising were part of the make up of the scene at the time

A typical shop layout which offered many bolt-on accessories. It showed how important customising was to scooter dealers financially

area to paint on and its far more exposed engine area which could be utilised. The T5 had been a huge influence on the street racer side and for a while, just after its introduction, it was the most popular choice. Piaggio's strange decision to phase it out and not bother with producing a successor was baffling to the whole industry. The P range was also going through design alterations and the majority found that they preferred the way it had looked before. The real threat now was that production of two-stroke engines would come to an end worldwide. If it did then the Vespa would only move further away from what it had been. Piaggio was still a going concern, selling to the masses, so a few thousand who liked the old style because it was easy to customise was of little concern. The other disadvantage that the Vespa had over the Lambretta was that many were still being used by scooterists as the reliable rally-going scooter. The supply of second-hand ones was now drying up.

When it came to the Lambretta, many new projects would start off as a bare frame and be built upwards. With the advent of mass-produced panels and engine casings from India – and a seemingly never-ending supply to boot – a project

Though people were now trying to save Lambrettas rather than cut them down, choppers such as this were still being built

was simple and cheap to start, certainly when it came to the GP which was the preferred choice for a custom scooter anyway.

There was no need to buy a good complete original example – and by this time these were starting to fetch huge premiums. Full custom scooters were not cheap to build so it didn't help if the initial outlay was expensive. Getting a cheaper frame and parts at the outset allowed more to be spent on the paint or the engine. The Vespa, on the other hand, was completely different as you had to start with a full machine in the first place. It was feared that the end of P range production altogether might push the price of older examples up. Therefore, with the original outlay of the scooter going up, the overall project became too costly to be worthwhile.

All this meant that the Lambretta would become the most popular choice when it came to building a custom scooter – certainly in the UK. The situation was different in other countries, including Germany, where strict road laws meant that the Lambretta was hardly used and that Vespa would continue to thrive. The custom scene in Europe was nowhere near as big, but some great well-engineered examples would be created as time went by. The Vespa would still be subject to customisation in the UK but the ratio against the Lambretta would be far lower. The fact that early PX examples were slowly being imported from Italy did help somewhat in getting the initial costs down. The problem was many were in good original condition and as they too were becoming rare many people didn't want to destroy that originality. Though there were far fewer custom Vespas being produced, there were some. Nevertheless, it would be the Lambretta that led the way.

With the start of a new millennium, everyone was thinking of a better future and that seemed true of the scooter scene. More dealers than ever were in business and all the subsidiaries that went along with it. Owners, it seemed, had even bigger disposable incomes and were keen to spend it on scooters. When the likes of Dazzle had first appeared, figures of £4000 were being quoted for its build cost. At the time it seemed almost unbelievable that so much would be spent on a scooter. Now paint jobs or engines on their own were costing as much if not more and the figure would only get higher. Even bare frames, especially those for the 200cc Lambrettas, were fetching four-figure sums.

It didn't deter people in the quest for perfection though and it seemed cost was irrelevant when it came to creating the perfect custom scooter. Soon a figure of £15,000 was deemed acceptable by those building them, whereas others would blame such creations for the general price of everything scooter-related going up. It was all a bit pie in the sky really and if someone wanted to have the best of everything in an engine it was going to cost a premium. If the next person wanted a more standard engine, it wasn't going to be any more expensive just because of this. It must be remembered that there were more dealers around now than before, so the competition was fierce and very competitive. If anything, the opposite was happening as it was bringing a lot of general costs down. A lot of the expense in building a custom scooter has always been due to the labour. If a person is spending many hours airbrushing a mural or engraving a side case, it's their time that is being paid for. The competition among the shops stopped anyone from overcharging for their services. Many kept their prices low for fear of losing custom to their rival down the road.

Those who wanted to build the best scooters just ignored the rumblings and rightly so. With the choice of components about to become even greater and the paint technology even better and more advanced, costs were only going to go upwards. More important is what was being created – and that was a good sign. The future of the custom scene was secure and it would continue to thrive. Now it was down to the owners to determine what direction it would take next.

Chapter Seven

A Work of Art

One of the main problems with any art form is that the longer it exists the more difficult it becomes to create something unique. Ideas that have never been seen before becoming less frequent. It then starts to become frustrating for those people concerned that what they are creating has been seen before or certainly something similar. If you look back at paintings throughout each century it's easy to see where styles changed and the methods used to create them. Perhaps in a way then the same could be said for the custom scooter. The real art of painting them with murals and images started back in the 1970s, several decades ago. Over that time the murals have changed, though not necessarily because the raw talent of the artists has changed.

The methods and equipment available have improved over that period and those doing the best job have kept up to date with those improvements. The competition has grown between artists just as it has between the owners who battle for supremacy. If a painter sees a scooter they have worked on winning at custom shows, it can be a huge boost to their trade. Demand for their services will grow – particularly if they come to be seen as among the best in the industry. Painting is a difficult job and the associated dust and fumes unleashed in enclosed spaces can result in an unpleasant working environment.

Consequently, over time, some have left the job because they no longer wish to put up with the conditions. Both the Vespa and Lambretta have a great many components, many of them difficult to work on, and painting it all can be rather laborious at times. And that's assuming that the components are in good shape. All too often, artists can be required to work with parts that are old and in poor condition – necessitating much preparation before painting can even begin.

Every time a custom scooter appeared with amazing paint or artwork it would wow the industry. This would set new standards and raise the benchmark even higher. It's this challenge for the next one to be even better that has led to continuous improvements in the standard of custom scooters. It also goes to show that it isn't just down to the owner how good the end result is. It's also down to the painter, engraver or anyone else involved in the process; it's a combined effort to make every part of the project absolute perfection. The same can be said of the fabricators coming up with a different piece of engineering to make something look even more radical and unique. Up until the Lambrettas of Jeremy Howlett appeared, ideas were based around existing components. He took it a step into the unknown by taking components and having them physically changed. They still had the same purpose but looked totally different from what had always been regarded as the norm. His creations were pioneering and proved just how far the custom concept could be taken. That's why everyone was in awe his creations when they came out because nothing like this had even been thought of before let alone seen.

Though it was difficult to come up with something new each time, ideas could always be improved on. The shock of seeing something different might get less and less over time but the ingenuity doesn't. Techniques improved and the painting process was a major part of that. Yet the reappearance of the same ideas time and again meant that the custom shows began to lose their sparkle somewhat.

People were becoming bored with seeing the same things. In a way this was understandable because it was the same format, a scooter painted, chromed, engraved, whatever. But the themes and the standard of workmanship only got better and that's probably what people didn't fully understand.

For a while, this created a slight lull, not in the building of scooters but in the platforms where they could be appreciated. Even the magazines were bombarded with letters asking for different types of scooters or articles to be featured. Some readers were now becoming tired of seeing wall to wall custom scooters. The scooter scene has always been fickle at the best of times and as the saying goes you can't please all the people all of the time. Getting both the magazines and the shows right started to become a bit of a balancing act but there

Stripping back to bare metal with a protective overlay to prevent rust has added a new style concept that is becoming more popular

A take on a widely used theme from the past that still works in the present day

The Lambretta SX 200 can look modern using the right colours, even if the scheme is retro

was never any question of custom scooters going away. Instead, there were just odd periods where things would quieten down a bit, perhaps with everyone taking a little breather.

Not helping the process was shortages of the basic raw material, the scooters themselves, not to mention their growing cost. The Lambretta had finished production more than 30 years ago by this time, while the Vespa T5 and the original P range had been gone for more than a decade. The Lambretta was beginning to fetch huge sums even for just a bare frame and engine, certainly with the 200cc models. One of the problems was that the direct-from-Italy source was beginning to dry up. This wasn't helped by a resurgence in interest of the Lambretta in Italy itself. With people starting to buy and restore them in the homeland of the Lambretta far fewer were now leaving the country. This was really beginning to push the price of the custom scooter to new heights.

By the time complete bodywork got to the painter and the engine to the builder, several thousand pounds had already been spent. Demand only seemed to be getting larger, adding to the problem. This was being driven by those who had got out of scooter ownership at the end of the 1980s and now wanted to relive their youth. With so much disposable income available and a lack of supply, prices were only going to get higher. It didn't seem to matter and as soon as a new ceiling was reached someone would pay more yet again for the same model. It also appeared that people weren't content with owning just one scooter either. It was no longer unusual for owners to have several, perhaps with a mix of both Lambrettas and Vespas.

The majority of those who were getting back into the scene just wanted to own a scooter once again. Some though were previous custom owners or builders and had the urge to create something amazing once again. It was a welcome boost to the trade and owners were discovering ideas and components that simply were not available when they were building their scooter the first time around. If a custom scooter was going to cost £20,000 to build, so what? It didn't matter. As the noughties progressed the rarest unrestored Lambrettas were fetching close to £10,000 and there was every reason to think that this point would soon be surpassed. That made spending a huge amount on a Lambretta seem much more acceptable. Even Vespas that were only 20 years old were seeing their value rise considerably.

Mixing many different custom styles and methods still works when used correctly

This was probably helped by the fact that the two-stroke as we knew it was finished. This was the strongest indication that the market was only going up not down.

Custom scooters started to follow certain patterns as the decade progressed. For the Vespa, it was based mainly around the P range as that was the accepted model best suited to alterations. Most of this was a throwback to the 1980s when

This Vespa PX uses subtle images without being too complicated to create a stunning look. Also reminding us of its past roots

Music is still one of the main inspirations for a custom theme with Northern Soul one of the most popular choices

The same can be said of bands still being a major influence

the type was at its peak. The days of the cutdown or chopper style using the P range seemed to be over though, probably due to the fact of their increasing rarity. There was the odd exception, but these were few and far between. The new trend, certainly for tuning, was with the small frame Vespa. Some of the big Vespa tuning houses were still producing hugely powerful kits and engines. This was because of a strong market based on racing and sprinting in mainland Europe.

Vespa street racers were now based around these engines and the small frame suited this style perfectly. Extremely powerful and lightweight, they were capable of over 100mph. Rivalry between owners of fast Vespas was building – who actually had the fastest one? As more were being built, they came with race paint and this helped to sustain interest in customisation. Quite often situations like this would came along and open up a new direction of customising. It didn't matter who was producing the engines, components or whatever, or whether it was for the Vespa or Lambretta. Anything that stirred things up was always welcome.

For the Lambretta that exact scenario was now being played out due to the scooter's huge resurgence in popularity. With so many new or re-enthused owners buying them up at such a fast rate, any company thinking of producing products for them knew that this was the time to do so. It all centred around performance and now there was an explosion of cylinder kits joining the market. These were not only from Europe but also the UK. It didn't matter whether it was small or

60s and 70s nostalgia can still find its way into the thinking of current custom ideas

large block engines – they were both catered for. A lot of this was down to modern engineering methods using computer aided design. This helped the design process of components to be made far more easily and using CNC machining helped bring down the tooling and production costs.

Now those with the ideas could implement them far more easily than they could have in the past. And it seemed many were prepared to do so judging by how much was now being produced specifically for the Lambretta. The power that was being quoted for these new kits was quite a remarkable way beyond anything that had previously been seen. They didn't disappoint either, with such kits as the RB manufactured by AF Rayspeed producing almost three times the power compared to when the engine had left the factory.

It was okay going fast, but this led to other problems. Stopping the machine became more important than ever – as did the suspension that had to cope with it. All of a sudden, all manner of products began to appear as the performance market for the Lambretta went into overdrive. Just as it had been with the small frame Vespa, the result was a street racer competition but on a much grander scale.

Moderate use of engraving without being too over the top, blended with custom paintwork on a Vespa. This proves that even after all these years the same methods can be used to create something fresh

The same idea used on a Lambretta, making it almost timeless in its design

As soon as a new kit was launched owners were having exclusive Lambrettas built dedicated to them. These would have just about every up to date product possible fitted to them, followed by complicated but colourful paint schemes. The focus was purely centred around racing and getting the desired look correct.

To go even one better, some owners were getting tuners to work on the latest cylinders to extract even more power. The simple reason was having the very best possible engine would make the whole thing stand out more. It was just as it had been in the 1980s when the likes of a Dave Webster Stage 6 engine was the must-have part for the top custom Lambrettas.

It didn't matter if the Lambretta concerned ever actually used the engine to its full potential – all that was important was that it had the capability to do so. It was all one-upmanship – an essential part of customising in and of itself – the fundamental desire to be different to everyone else. News broke towards the end of the decade that there would be a purpose-built engine for the Lambretta, raising the bar even higher. Not only that but it would also be a twin-cylinder project. Building a huge engine like this didn't come at a cheap price and estimates of around £9000

Themes can still come from almost anything but they work when done right

were being bandied around – an eye-watering amount. Even if this was fitted into the cheapest model, the resulting machine's value would be pushed into five figures. And given that it was much more likely to be fitted to a rarer and more expensive model, the cost would probably be considerably greater. By the time all the extras were added as well as a paint job to suit and the labour costs involved building it,

The classic lines of the AF S Type, one of the most copied styles ever but one that will never go out of fashion

there was the possibility of it costing over £25,000. Yet even this failed to deter some, who began making plans for just such a scooter to be built.

The Lambretta had changed somewhat when it came to customisation, just as the Vespa had. Most were built around the full-frame and body idea, leaving behind the chopper and cutdown era. Some of these would still be built, but it was never going to be like it was back in the 1980s. The rarity and cost of a Lambretta made it a far less attractive proposition. However, at the end of the

The modern Lambretta street racer using the latest technology but a layout that has been around for several decades

day if the owner wanted to cut the back end off an SX 200 it was their choice to do so and no one could put a stop to it. Yet by doing so they would considerably reduce their scooter's value and that's what really stopped people from taking those steps.

There was an answer to this problem though because there was a huge supply of Indian Lambrettas still being imported into the UK. These had value, true, but nothing like that of the original Italian examples and they were very much seen as the cheaper alternative. Cutting down or extensively modifying an Indian frame wasn't a problem because it wasn't so costly. Some purists held the argument that an Indian Lambretta simply wasn't the same. It didn't really matter to the majority though because they still saw it as a Lambretta, which it was. To prove the point some of the top customer Lambretta creations were now Indian because they were the ones being extensively engineered and modified.

By 2010 it was more than 50 years since the customisation of both makes had started. There had been more intense periods, like in the 1980s, and times before and after where it had gone out of fashion. One way or another it had continued

**Time Trouble and Money, still in its original condition from the 1980s.
Though it has the odd mark here and there, altering it would be sacrilege**

and showed no signs of ever dying out. The same could be said for the rest of the
industry that supported it. From the skilled painters to the entrepreneurs producing
aftermarket products, there was no sign of the scene abating. So much was now
being produced it was almost as easy to build a complete Lambretta from scratch
as it had been when they were still in production. Similarly, entrant numbers at
rallies and custom shows were still big enough to warrant putting such events on
and the crowds would still pay to come and see them.

The standards kept on improving but there was no denying that many harked
back to what was seen as the golden period. When it came to generating new
ideas, many looked to the past for inspiration. No one was directly copying custom
scooters from an earlier period though – there was no need to. If anything, it was
only the methods such as engraving or painting styles that were used as an example.
Themes would come in and out of fashion just like anything in this world does, but
slowly retro based ideas were creeping into the current builds. Just like the classic
street racers of the late 1980s which were a throwback to a time 20 years earlier.

One of the most famous mod scooters from the 1960s rediscovered and restored to its former glory. An important part of scooter custom history that has thankfully been saved

And there was another angle to all this that people were beginning to think about even more. Instead of copying custom scooters from the past, why not rejuvenate them instead? A lot of machines built back in the day still belonged to the original owners. They may have been updated or revamped, Italian Stallion and Sign of the Snake being good examples, and they were still around. Many though had either been destroyed or left to deteriorate when their original owner moved on to something else. Some of them had been sold and since rebuilt and resprayed. Some of the originals did still exist though and with the advent of social media were rediscovered. Those that remained and could be bought were quickly snapped up regardless of their condition. Even those that had been kept in good storage had usually been lying idle for a considerable amount of time. Their bodywork might be okay but most had started to rust. As for the engine on such a find, it would definitely be in need of a rebuild.

The original Supertune Lowline from 1967 thought lost forever but recently discovered and renovated. Probably one of the most important examples of early scooter customisation still in existence

The question next arose of how far someone should go when bringing a scooter back to its former glory. The answer depended a lot of what there was to work with. If the engine, for instance, had been used and abused, then items such as the cylinder and crank might need replacing. The problem was, some items were simply not available any more. If the intention was to just save the scooter and not use it then it wasn't an issue. If it was to be put back on the road though, modern-day replacements would be needed. No one was suggesting it had to use the same tyres it was built with or its original clutch plates – which by this time would have perished anyway. If the scooter itself was kept as original as possible then it was accepted that the running gear at least would probably have to be replaced.

Depending on whether the chrome had peeled or gone rusty then getting it re-done was also perfectly acceptable. Just like paintwork that might have been stone chipped or scratched. Anyway, the likelihood of rust meant that, as a bare minimum, getting it professionally touched up was fine. Some bodywork may have needed totally redoing, such as a whole side panel, but if that meant the difference between saving a machine or not then it had to be done. There were the odd exceptions where scooters whose bodywork was in fairly good condition were simply cleaned up to preserve originality. Odd marks only added to the patina and proved that the scooter hadn't been tampered with in any way shape or form.

The knock-on effect was to create another style within the scene. Now instead of building custom scooters from scratch people were renovating old ones. It created big interest and proved just how much of a deep history the custom scooter scene now had.

There were only going to be so many old custom scooters found though as some were lost forever. That didn't matter as long as those that were found got into the right hands and were saved. It had also become apparent that some had gone abroad when the original owners had decided to sell. Most that did leave the UK ended up in Europe and possibly a few went to Japan when the Japanese were buying up UK scooters in the early 1990s. Germany seemed to be the epicentre for all this and slowly many scooters began to resurface there. When it transpired that a lot of Jeremy Howlett's Lambrettas had been saved and still resided in the UK, this was major news. Dazzle, which was the most famous because it was his first creation, began a painstaking restoration. It sparked huge interest throughout the scootering community and even Howlett himself took the opportunity to reunite with it again at its first showing.

The Lambretta still remained the number one choice when it came to customising. The Vespa had its place and would always be there, but it was never going to be how it was in the past. Part of the reason was down to the Vespa still being in production. Though the aftermarket for the P range did exist, big manufacturers would concentrate on producing parts for the more modern machines rather than the old ones. No one could blame them as that was where the lucrative business was.

Totally the opposite was happening with the Lambretta. There had been a huge number of products made with some costing a considerable amount with tooling costs. Regardless, it didn't stop even more from entering the market. Some feared it may have got to saturation point and that if they invested at this stage they may never see a return on their money, perhaps even making a loss. Somehow that just didn't happen and this was good news for the custom scene. Just like when this resurgence had first started, creating competition among owners, it was still showing no signs of slowing down.

Chapter Eight

The Trend Will Live Forever

As long as there is a supply of both the Lambretta and Vespa then the scooter scene will always remain. Some people may retire from riding them or the number of scooters on the road may decline from natural wastage. There may also be threats from the government in trying to ban all petrol engines in years to come. Yet the scooter scene will never die out completely – certainly not in our lifetime. Even if they are eventually banned from the road, scooters will still be built and possibly custom ones too, taking the scene over to a certain extent. For now though, regardless of the thinly veiled threats, it remains strong.

Competition to produce the best scooter whatever style its created in hasn't changed in the slightest and if anything, only gets stronger. The rivalry at shows is just as intense, with new unveilings at the beginning of the season – ready to do battle with each other throughout the year for the top accolades. Despite the show circuit still being strong, a new trend has begun to emerge. Not everyone, it seems, enters their scooter at shows. Many are now happy to build them to a high standard just to be used on the road. Quite often a custom scooter can go almost unnoticed by the majority until it is photographed somewhere. What this proves is that the custom scene isn't purely about shows and winning trophies. There's nothing wrong with that and without it the scene wouldn't have grown into what it is. But now there is another side to it all.

There are those who want their scooters in the limelight and those who don't. Together both are making a strong force for the future. The ideas and the creations still continue to flow, even if the shock aspect has perhaps thinned out a little. The different aspects that make it all up have more than likely been fully explored with no new avenues to go down. But that alone will never be enough to stop scooter owners striving for the next idea of perfection or individualism.

Though there is still the opportunity for someone to create a totally unique scooter, the real focus is on the finished look whatever style it's in.

Creating a custom scooter is a very individual thing and no two are ever the same. An owner can have an idea sitting in their mind for years before taking the

A modern auto engine fitted into a Lambretta frame – a modern way of building a street racer

An old Vespa GS can still create a stunning full-blown custom scooter. The Lambretta GP, over 50 years old, will always have that option

The Menace proving new ideas are always possible

The 1960s look will always have its place within the custom scene, however outlandish it may be. Similarly, so too will the 1970s look. As for the 1980s – that remains as strong as ever

Metalflake and chrome are still major ingredients of the legendary S Type

Racing scooters will forever influence the street racer. Not forgetting the variations of Formula 1 and other aspects of motorsport

Films will also continue to be an inspiration

Legends such as Wake and Dazzle forever preserved, reminding us of where the true custom scooter came from

But the biggest influence of all is simply how far we can expand the thoughts of our minds

plunge and building it. That doesn't matter one bit – what does is that their dream comes to fruition and the scooter is created. It's this individualism that still exists today and that means the art will never die out. No one has ever been able to explain why the scooter scene is the way it is and they probably never will. There is certainly nothing else in the world like it. After more than 60 years since it all started, the custom scooter has its place firmly centred in the middle of it all and always will.

Chapter Nine

Gallery

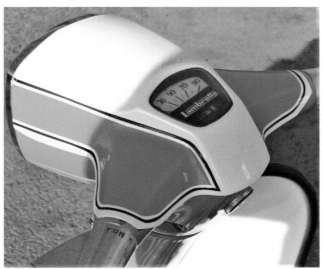